THE
BIRD HOUSE
BOOK

A Sterling/Lark Book
Sterling Publishing Co., Inc. New York

Editing: Thom Boswell
Design & Production: Thom Boswell
Typesetting: David Schoonmaker
        and Elaine Thompson
Photography: Evan Bracken
Instructional Drawings: Don Osby

684.08
WOO

ISBN 0-8069-8324-8 (Hardback)

Woods, Bruce, 1947-
  The bird house book : how to build fanciful bird
houses and feeders, from the purely practical to
the absolutely outrageous / Bruce Woods &
David Schoonmaker.
        p.   cm.
   "A Sterling/Lark book"--T.p. verso.
   Includes bibliographical
      references and index.
   ISBN 0-8069-8324-8
   1. Birdhouses--Design and construction.
   2. Bird feeders--Design and construction.
I. Schoonmaker, David. II. Title. III. Title: The
Bird House Book.
QL678.5.W65   1991
690'.89--dc20   90-24289
                          9/92   CIP

A Sterling/Lark Book

Text by Bruce Woods and
      David Schoonmaker

Produced by Altamont Press, Inc.
50 College Street, Asheville, NC 28801

Published in 1991 by Sterling Publishing Co., Inc.
      387 Park Avenue S., NY, NY 10016

© 1991 Altamont Press

Distributed in Canada by Sterling Publishing
c/o Canadian Manda Group, PO Box 920, Station U
      Toronto, Ontario, Canada M8Z 5P9
Distributed in the United Kingdom by Cassell PLC
      Villers House, 41/47 Strand, London
      WC2N 5JE, England
Distributed in Australia by Capricorn, Ltd.,
      P.O. Box 665, Lane Cove, NSW 2066

Every effort has been made to ensure that all information in this book is accurate. However, due
to differing conditions, tools, and individual skills, the publisher cannot be responsible for any
injuries, losses, or other damages which may result from the use of the information in this book.

THE BIRD HOUSE BOOK

How to Build
Fanciful Bird Houses and Feeders,
from the Purely Practical to the
Absolutely Outrageous

Bruce Woods & David Schoonmaker

Table of

The Bird Houses

Contents

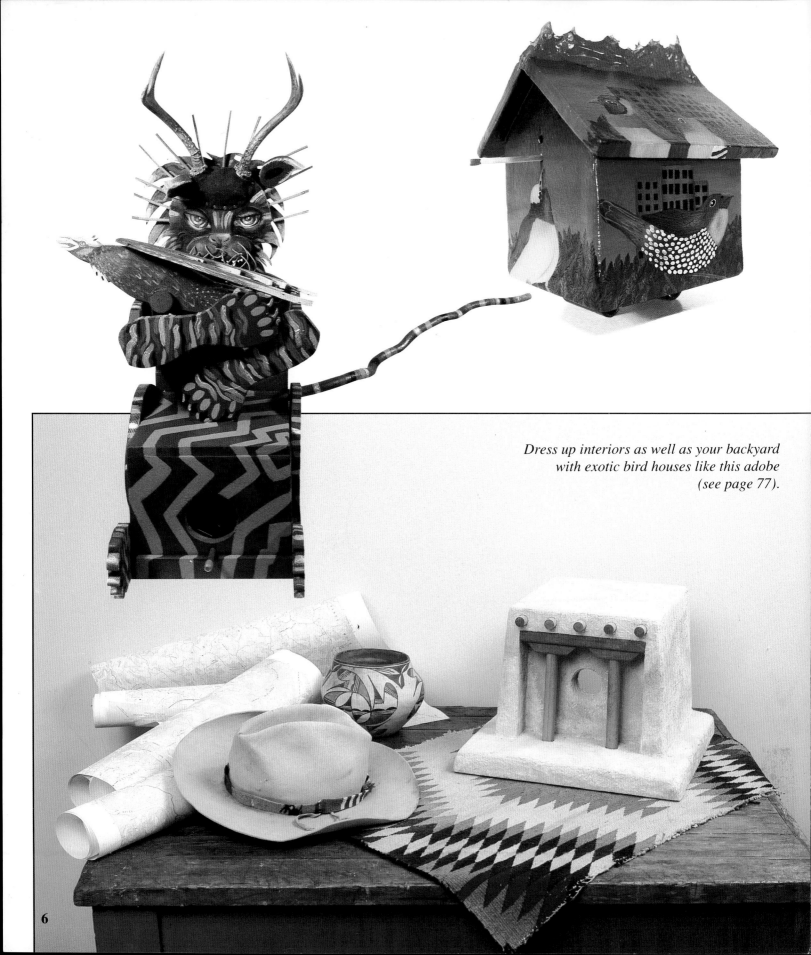

Dress up interiors as well as your backyard with exotic bird houses like this adobe (see page 77).

6

Artful bird houses exhibited at the Wustum Museum in Racine, Wisconsin.

While not included in the instructional section of this book, bird houses such as these transcend functionalism, achieving the status of fine art.

Introduction

Welcome to The Bird House Book. Should you be surreptitiously scanning through these pages prior to purchasing, you will have noticed that this is, more than anything, a book on building bird houses (or nesting boxes, to use the more technical term). You will also have noted that the designs herein range from the simplest of "Lapwing Levittown" cubicles to the most fanciful of martin mansions. And you might have wondered, knowing that even the most basic of these projects will consume some time and expense, just why do people build bird houses, anyway.

Funny you should ask.

The practice of crafting shelters for nesting wildfowl isn't a new one. In fact, its roots go well back into both North American and European history. Members of some Native American tribes hung hollow gourds to attract nesting purple martins, just as many bird enthusiasts do today. (Our version of this venerable design appears on page 39.) Audubon claimed that the territorial martins were valued because they'd drive away turkey vultures which might otherwise dine off the Indians' meat racks when the tribe was away. In Europe of the middle ages, however, bird houses were erected out of an even purer pragmatism; the fledgling starlings and sparrows born therein were regularly gathered and eaten. (Modern bird-housekeepers who may be bothered by these two "pest" species might consider this solution a particularly unpleasant form of swallowing one's pride!)

A great many nest boxes are still built for eminently practical reasons. Gardeners, for example, have always waged war with insect pests. And, in recent years, we've become more and more aware that many of the chemical weapons we've come to rely upon do far more harm than good. So, in the interest of environmental responsibility, many flower and vegetable growers have turned again to mankind's oldest allies in this struggle: the birds. A great many of the avian species that will happily nest in man-made structures are first-rate exterminators. Robins, wrens, thrushes, war-

Turned wood bird house sculpture by Andy Barnum.

blers and swallows will all gladly patrol any potato patches near their happy homes. In fact, the nearer the better. If you've ever watched the eating habits of fledglings (use binoculars, please; never approach close enough to nesting birds to disturb them), you'll know that a short flight between bountiful bugs and waiting beaks is a bird parent's dream come true.

And, as you may know, the purple martin's appetite for flying insects is legendary. Although his reputed ability to control mosquitos may be somewhat more legend than fact (since martins hunt in the daytime, and skeeters tend to prowl in the dark), these beautiful aerobats certainly do account for some mosquitos at dusk, and keep a check on the hoards of various other flying insect species day in and day out.

As an aside, it's interesting to note that birds have come to function as early warning systems in the face of environmental hazards. Just as a caged canary in a coal mine provides the first signs of potentially deadly gas, so our feathered friends have given us early notice of the hazards of chemical pesticides (as noted in Rachael Carson's Silent Spring), and have also provided some of the best alternatives to these poisons!

Of course, many a backyard bird house builder acts in the interests of amateur science. Bird watching (or "birding") is a well-established and increasingly popular activity . . . especially in the U.S. and the British Isles. Birders are apt to approach their house-building very seriously, to provide habitat for species that have been denied their usual nest sites by advancing civilization, or to lure species back into a range they'd abandoned. Whether their sport centers on the compilation of a "life list" of species (as is the case with many American birders) or of the collection of extensive field notes and observations (the more typical European/English form of this pastime), amateur bird watchers provide a valuable "citizen's ornithology corps", and increase both our understanding of avian behavior and our ability to design nesting boxes to serve specific species.

A working bird house made of non-traditional materials by Steve Bishop.

Bird house structure by Dennis Markley.

The aspiring bird house builder can find inspiration in these four functional designs by Randy Sewell, suitable for post-mounting.

A totem-like housing complex by Laura Foreman.

"Aviatrix Series/Techno-Birds," by Thomas Mann (opposite).

A related group (though it might shock some birders to hear it said) are the hunter/conservationists who work to preserve wetland habitat for waterfowl and who build and distribute wood duck houses. It's become somewhat fashionable to look down one's nose at nimrods, but the fact remains that no other single conservation group has raised as much money for the preservation of wild habitat as has been collected through the various taxes on rifles, shotguns, ammunition, and so forth bought by U.S. hunters. Furthermore, a great many of these sportsmen and women are both fascinated by and knowledgeable about game and non-game species alike, and are eager to bring as much of the wild into their own backyards as they can.

Many a bird house builder, though, could care little which species takes up residence in his or her creation. This sort of landlord is overjoyed by any tenant, and can take as much pleasure in the antics of the common sparrow as in the shock of color that announces a nesting bluebird. It seems that all of us have the urge to "get back to the Garden", and a lucky few can even hear the airs of Eden in the whistles of the starling.

Finally, there's the bird house builder who's creations will probably never see the out-of-doors. This craftsperson will, we hope, be inspired by the fanciful nest boxes in our later pages. He or she loves the precise miniaturization of the dollhouse, the clean simplicity of rustic design, and the playfulness of outrageous creations. In many cases, these "houses" are most certainly not "homes" (in fact, you probably couldn't bait a bird into some of the more extreme designs), but they most certainly are fine examples (be they whimsical or overwhelming) of the woodworker's skill and the architect-in-miniature's imagination.

Why build bird houses? For all of the above reasons, and then some. And probably most of all for the oldest reason of all: to use our hands to take something from the mind and make it real, to feel the satisfaction that only comes from creation. Come on, let's get building!

13

These two rustic creations from Garden Source illustrate how elaborate facades can embellish livable bird chambers (see page 44 for basic construction techniques).

Natural History

Given the options open to them in the natural world, it could be said that birds aren't particularly choosy about their living quarters. After all, most of us have heard of (or seen) species taking up residence in such unlikely abodes as mailboxes, drain spouts, and even the tailpipes of abandoned automobiles.

Still, and perhaps surprisingly, most bird species are difficult (or virtually impossible) to lure into man-made housing. And, of those that will move into bird houses or nest platforms, most have rather specific requirements for house size, hole diameter, placement, and so forth. Since you'll have a better chance of attracting a specific species if you build to suit its particular tastes, the following chart details the specifications for bird houses suitable for most of the more common house-nesting birds of North America and the British Isles. There are, of course, house-nesters that we haven't included. To determine how to build a structure to suit their needs, take into consideration the size of the bird (use the dimensions below that suit a comparable species), its preferred habitat (which will give you a clue to appropriate siting), and the character of the nests it builds in the wild (birds that build pen nests on tree limbs and the like will prefer a nesting platform; those that occupy holes in trees or cliff-sides will more likely be attracted to an enclosure).

And remember, too, that the following guidelines are simply that. Bird house design is not an exact science. Your own ongoing observations of birds will certainly teach you tricks not noted here. Further, a bird house should please the builder as well as the hoped-for tenant. As some of the designs detailed later in this book attest, the most pleasing bird houses to build may, for some craftspeople, be those that decorate their living rooms, and that serve only as objects of art or whimsy, far from the flight paths of our feathered friends.

Indian Hawk

A pine bark and thatch bird dwelling by English Thatch.

Some House-Nesting Birds

SPECIES	APPROXIMATE DIMENSIONS	HOLE DIMENSIONS
BLUEBIRD (Eastern, Western, and Mountain)[1] Sialia spp.	Floor: 5" x 5" Interior height: 8" to 10"	Height above floor (centered): 6" (5" Diameter: 1-1/2" for Warbler)
CHICKADEE (Black-capped, Boreal, and Carolina)[2] Parus spp.	Floor: 4" x 4" Interior height: 8" to 10"	Height above floor (centered): 6" Diameter: 1-1/4"
FINCH (House and Purple) Carpodacus spp.	Floor: 6" x 6" Interior height: 6"	Height above floor (centered): 3"-4" Diameter: 2"
FLICKER Colaptes auratus	Floor: 7" x 7" Interior hieght: 16"+	Height above floor (centered): 12"+ Diameter: 2-3/4"
FLYCATCHER (Many varieties) Tyrannus spp., Myiarchus spp.	Floor: 6" x 6" Interior height: 14"	Height above floor (centered): 6"+ Diameter: 2"
JACKDAW (Corvus moredula)	Floor: 8" x 8" Interior height 12"	Height above floor (centered): 6" Diameter: 6"
OWL (Barn) Tyto alba	Floor: 10" x 18" Interior height: 18"	Height above floor (centered): 4" Diameter: 6"
OWL (Saw-whet, Screech and Little) Aegolius acadicus, Otus asio and Athene noctua	Floor: 10" x 10" Interior height: 15"	Height above floor (centered): 10"+ Diameter: 3"
PIGEON (Street) Columba livia	Floor: 8" x 8" Interior height; 8"	Height above floor (centered): 4" Diameter: 4"
PURPLE MARTIN (Progne subus)	Floor: 6" x 6" Interior height: 6" (each compartment)	Height above floor (centered): 1-3/4" Diameter: 2-1/2"
ROBIN (American and English)[3] Tardus migratorius and Erithacus rubecula	Floor: 6" x 6" Interior height: 8" (open roofed platform)	No hole, open-sided roofed box
SPARROWS (House and many others) Passer domesticus, members of Family Fringillidae	Floor: 10" x 10" Interior height: 15"+	Height above floor (centered): 6" Diameter: 1-1/2"
WOOD DUCK[4] Aix sponsa	Floor: 6"x 6" Interior height: 14"+	Height above floor (centered): 12"- 16" (9"-12" for Kestrel) Diameter: 3" x 4" (oval)
WOODPECKER (Hairy, Red-bellied, Red-cockaded, Red-headed, and Yellow-bellied Sapsucker) Picoides villosus, Melanerpes carolinus, Picoides borealis, Melanerpes erythrocephalus, and Sphyrapicus varius	Floor: 8" x 8" Interior height: 24"	Height above floor (centered): 9"-12" Diameter: 1-1/2" (Hairy, Red-bellied, Red-cockaded, Sapsucker) 2" (Red-headed)
WOODPECKER (Pileated) Dryocopus pileatus	Floor: 4" x 4" Interior height: 14"	Height above floor (centered): 10" Diameter: 4"
WRENS (House, Bewick's, Carolina, and others) Family Troglodytidae	Floor: 4" x 4" Interior Height: 8"	Height above floor (centered): 4" Diameter: 1-1/4" (House) 1-1/2 (Bewick's, Carolina, and others)

[1]House will also serve: Tree Swallow (Iridoprocne bicolor), Warblers (Parula spp.), Spotted Flycatcher (Muscicapa striata)

[2]House will also serve: Brown Creeper (Certhia familiaris), Downy Woodpecker (Picoides pubescens), Nuthatches (Sitta spp.), Tufted Titmouse (parus bicolor)

HEIGHT ABOVE GROUND	SITING TIPS	SUITABLE HOUSES
5'-10'	On fence posts, stumps, utility poles, tree trunks, etc. Place around open fields or any grassy expanse (park, cemetary, golf course). Predator collar suggested.	Pages 57, 64, 69, 73, 75, 96
6'-15"	Locate near large trees. Line with non-aromatic wood shavings.	41, 42, 51, 52, 75
8'-12'	Both birds primarily Western though sometimes found in East. Purple Finch prefers wooded site.	59, 64, 66, 77, 101
6'-20'	Site on tree trunk, line bottom with 3"+ of non-aromatic sawdust.	42, 57, 64, 92, 109
8'-20'	Prefers wooded site, natural-appearing house.	42, 83, 92, 109
10'+	Away from human noise.	66, 86, 92
12'-20'	Locate near open fields/meadows to provide hunting range.	48
10'-30'	Near water if at all possible. Prefers open yard with few or no trees nearby.	66, 83, 86
10'+	Prefers a perch.	42, 66, 83, 86, 92
Above reach of cats	Prefers open area near well-maintained lawns for feeding.	39, 79, 89, 105
12'	Habitats vary widely.	55, 61, 114
10'-20'	Locate on trees or buildings.	66, 83, 86, 92
12'-20'	Wood Duck: Locate near (or above) water, line with 3"+ non aromatic sawdust, predator collar suggested. Kestrel: Site on edge of field or meadow to provide hunting range.	42, 64, 66, 109
12'-20'	Site on tree trunk, much prefers natural-looking house (bark lined, for example).	41, 42, 66
6'-10'	Locate among large trees. Natural-looking house essential.	41, 42, 64, 75, 109
6'-10'	Site on edge of woods, in fencerows, etc.	41, 42, 52, 59, 75, 96

[3]House (nesting platform) will also serve: Barn Swallow (Riparia riparia), Phoebes, Eastern and Say's (Sayornis spp.), Various Thrushes (Cartharus spp.), Song Sparrow (Mclospiza melodia),Pied Wagtail (Motacilla alba)

[4]House will also serve: American Kestrel (Falco sparvarius), European Kestrel (Falco tinnunculus)

Unwanted Guests

In the best of all possible worlds, our bird houses and feeders would only attract the most beautiful, entertaining and musical species, and our backyards would soon be woven into a tapestry of color and sound, an avian Utopia created by human hands. That's never the case in the real world, however. Bird houses that we hope will shelter rare bluebirds or clownish woodpeckers suffer the invasions of unwanted house sparrows and starlings. Feeders are ravaged by gluttonous squirrels, and both feeding and nesting birds—as well as eggs and fledglings—can attract the unwanted attention of cats, dogs, skunks and raccoons . . . not to mention such predatory bird species as shrikes and hawks.

Yes, your backyard *is* a jungle. But there are steps that can be taken to tame it, and to lessen (but not eliminate) the impact of unwanted guests.

Sparrows

House sparrows *love* bird houses, and they're not overly picky about the neighborhood they find their dwellings in. They *do*, however, prefer to perch before they enter. Bluebirds (and many other "desirable" species) can enter a hole without stopping to look it over. If you want to keep sparrows out of your bird houses, leave the perches off.

Sparrows like nothing better than bellying up to a feeder, too. The best solution would probably be to provide enough feeders, and feed, for everyone. (After all, sparrows are fascinating to watch and really quite attractive. They merely suffer the contempt of familiarity.) If you'd rather not feed the little ruffians at all, though, stock your platform with Niger thistle, peanuts, and red proso millet. Sparrows tend to turn their beaks up at all three.

Starlings

Like the English Sparrow, the European Starling is a non-indigenous species. (They were actually introduced into North America as part of a plan to stock the continent with all of the birds mentioned in the writings of Shakespeare!) Unfortunately, there's no simple way to keep starlings out of your bird houses. Your best bet is to follow the dimensions given in the House-Nesting chart (pages 16 & 17) religiously, and then try to maintain a philosophical attitude when starlings take up residence anyway! (After all, a Bard in the hand . . . .)

At the feeder, starlings will be primarily suet-eaters. A seed-filled feeder will hold little interest for them. If you want to attract insect-eaters such as woodpeckers, wrens and creepers, though, you might as well put up enough suet to feed the starlings, too.

Cats

Cats aren't stupid. And a low bird feeder or bath, especially if it's conveniently situated near some good stalking cover, is about as close to a free lunch as the average itinerant feline could hope for . . . unless you consider a front-row seat beneath a bird house when early flying lessons are going on!

If you have cats yourself, you might consider belling them if their territory overlaps your back yard bird sanctuary. (Make sure the belled collar will slip or break free should it get caught in brush, though.) You can also cool cats by mowing around feeders, siting feeders and houses above easy leaping range, and even hanging the structures on metal poles or installing a conical predator collar, as shown on page 37. In extreme cases it's even possible to fence around low feeders or fledgling-filled houses with chicken wire.

Dogs

Old Blue's intentions may be the best in the world, but if he spends his afternoons scratching and drooling in your backyard, you can bet that you'll be hanging a lot of vacancy signs on nearby bird houses. If a neighbor's dog makes a pest of itself, you can A) yell at it, B) yell at the neighbor (but be warned, "dog feuds" can easily escalate all out of proportion!), or C) fence it out. Again, most canines won't actively bother feeding or nesting birds, but their very presence will make the more timid species keep their distance.

Raccoons, Skunks, Opossum, etc.

A lot of creatures eat birds (just ask Colonel Sanders), and, especially if you're lucky enough to live in the country, a wide range of wild mammals may be waiting to turn your aviary into a smorgasbord. Follow the prevention steps suggested for discouraging cats. Wild mammals can also be live-trapped (in a Hav-a-hart brand or similar box trap) and transported away from your property, or—should your inclinations bend that way—even shot. (Check with your local fish and game department before taking drastic action, though, and don't attempt to shoot anything unless you know how to kill it cleanly and know that the rifle or shotgun and ammunition you're using are adequate for the job.)

Hawks and Shrikes

Some of the more tenderhearted of birders might consider us a bit cold-blooded, but we figure that a backyard that manages to attract one of these predatory birds is pretty darned lucky! It would be hard to imagine the kind of mass attack by hawks or shrikes that would be necessary to clean out a feeder or nesting area, and a few random predations offer a rare opportunity to view some of the most terribly beautiful aspects of wild bird behavior. Don't worry about hawks or shrikes destroying the scene you've carefully set, appreciate the drama they bring to it.

Squirrels

There are stories of owners of bird feeders being locked into battles with individual squirrels that last for decades and consume thousands of dollars. You *can* keep squirrels out of your bird feeder . . . all you have to do is place it atop a slick metal post at least thirty feet from the nearest tree limb. If that's not an alternative, try the various baffles and do-dads on the market. Then, if your squirrels outwit all of them (as ours have), set out a separate squirrel station featuring whole cobs of dried feed corn. You just might find yourself spending as much time watching the antics of your furred visitors as you do eying the feathered action a tree or two away.

In fact, that may be the main lesson to be learned about the darker side of the bird feeder/bird house game: there are few perfect worlds, even for the birds. Control the problems that you *can* solve, modify your aspirations when you're left with no choice, and—no matter what—be open to learning and taking enjoyment from the growth of the dynamic community that, though you may have brought it into being, is really most successful when it's beyond your control.

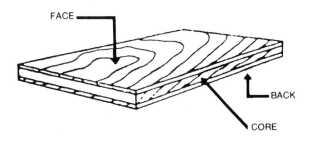

THREE-PLY VENEER CORE CONSTRUCTION

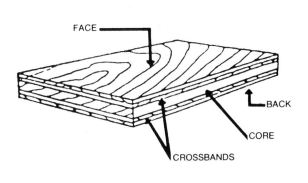

FIVE-PLY VENEER CORE CONSTRUCTION

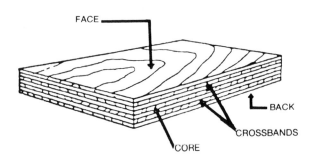

MULTI-PLY VENEER CORE CONSTRUCTION

Materials

No ultimate material exists for building birdhouses. The right combination for your birdhouse will be determined by your climate, the design, the availability of products at the local lumberyard or hardware store, and the way you balance the depth of your pocketbook with the life span of the birdhouse.

Moisture is the worst enemy of every part of a birdhouse. If you're fortunate enough to live in a dry climate, you can build your birdhouse out of darn near anything and expect it to last decades. Desert residents, for example, will do better devoting attention to choosing finishes that can withstand the ravages of intense ultraviolet radiation. Most of us, however, should consider water first when we choose materials and pick designs.

Any wood that stays damp will rot eventually, though some species resist fungal attacks better than others, and oxidation affects every metal to some degree. In the following paragraphs we'll describe several weather-resistant commercial woods and discuss fasteners and adhesives suited to damp environments, but, as the old saw goes, an ounce of prevention . . . . People who live in damp climates should use weather-resistant materials *and* be wary of designs with platforms or other exposed horizontal sections.

Manufactured Lumber

Assuming that you plan to build your birdhouse from wood, your first major material choice is between manufactured and solid lumber. Laminated and amalgamated wood products are gaining popularity while quality solid lumber becomes more difficult (and expensive) to find. As this book goes to press, however, marine- or exterior-grade plywood and oriented stand board remain the only manufactured lumber products suitable for birdhouses. Other solid-wood substitutes either lack weather resistance or contain urea-formaldehyde glues that may be offensive to, or unhealthful for, birds.

In comparison with solid lumber, manufactured lumber boasts the advantages of strength, economy, availability in a variety of thicknesses, and dimensional stability—that is, it expands and contracts little with temperature and humidity and isn't prone to warp. On the other hand, it requires powertools with special blades and bits for smooth cutting and drilling, and particular attention to sealing its end grain, which is exposed on all four sides.

When you shop for plywood, be sure to specify marine or, at the least, exterior grade. Both plywoods are laminated with waterproof glues; marine has the advantage of having no voids (knot holes allowed in inner laminations of many plywoods), which makes it much easier to join and results in less waste. Don't be distracted by the pretty oak or birch veneer plywoods you may find in the cabinetmaker's department; they won't stand up to outdoor life. Your lumberyard sales person might suggest pressure-treated plywood for a birdhouse. We do not. Though wood that has been treated with chromated copper arsenate (often called salt treated or by the acronym CCA) resists decay very well and isn't hazardous in most applications, it doesn't belong in a birdhouse any more than it does in a baby's crib. Tiny, pecking birds are far more likely to get a dangerous dose of heavy metals than people sitting in chairs on a deck made of treated lumber.

Marine plywood is pretty much standardized, though you might find some specialty mills offering marine grades with additional laminations (nice for fancy boats but entirely unnecessary for birdhouses). Structural exterior plywoods are graded by letters, according to the quality of each face. C-D, for example, is crude sheathing commonly used underneath shingles on a roof. Luckily, no F plywood exists. You'll probably prefer A-C or B-C, which offers one face with an excellent or very good finish and a lesser-quality side for the birds, which won't be offended. Few birdhouses need more than 3/8" plywood for strength. In general, 1/4" is fine for the smaller houses, while 3/8" is better for the larger ones. However, you may find a wider variety of grades in 1/2".

In the Materials Lists that accompany each bird house, types of plywood will not be specified. You can choose as you see fit.

Oriented strand board is a relatively recent development and shouldn't be confused with nonstructural materials such as particle board and flake board. OSB is routinely available in 1/4", 3/8", 1/2", and 3/4" thickness. There are no grades. When we have used OSB in a bird house, it will be specified in the Materials List.

Materials

Solid Lumber

Many birdhouse builders still choose solid lumber, perhaps as much for aesthetic reasons as for practical ones. Many woodworkers find wood with closer family ties to trees to be more pleasant and forgiving to work, and aesthetically, it's the only choice for most projects that will receive a clear finish to expose the wood's grain. Solid wood's major liability is that, other than moldings, it's routinely available only in 3/4" and greater thicknesses. That's far thicker than necessary for a petite 6"-square birdhouse and may look ungainly, for example, on the roof of a design that imitates a human house. Unless you have access to a thickness planer, you'll have to live with this limitation or mix boards and plywood to get the right proportions.

Several species are naturally resistant to decay, and you should use these materials on any face that lies within 10° of horizontal or that has an horizontal joint exposed to the weather. On most designs, that will include only the floor and the walls that intersect it. For other reasons, though, you may want to use one of the woods in the following section exclusively. For example, dimensions in different species of lumber often differ slightly, which could complicate accurate joinery. Besides, you may find these woods very pleasant to work with, and the additional expense for a small birdhouse is minimal.

Commercial weather-resistant solid wood species include cedar, cypress, redwood, and a variety of tropical woods. Of these, western-red cedar is the most widely available and economical. It's also lightweight and easy to cut.

However, some birds—chickadees, for example—may be put off by its strong aroma. Likewise, some humans react to cedar with symptoms such as nasal and eye irritation, a problem compounded during sawing, drilling, or sanding. Old-growth cypress has lovely grain and durable heartwood but often splinters when nailed. Clear-heart redwood works wonderfully and can be found at most quality lumberyards, but costs at least twice as much as cedar. Of the tropical woods, banak is the most widely available. It is a reddish-brown, medium-density wood that is very stable and rot resistant. About the only caveat worth mentioning, besides the environmental one concerning rain forest devastation (fortunately, most commercial banak is grown on plantations) is that the wood's open grain makes it difficult to finish to a smooth surface. Happily, noncommercial species renowned for decay resistance abound. Locally you may find yew, osage orange, black locust, or others.

If you do use conventional lumber—whether for the frame of the birdhouse or for trim—don't try to skimp by using lesser grades. Knots and other imperfections are very difficult to deal with in the sort of small-scale woodworking projects described in this book. Either buy better grades in the first place, or trim out all the imperfections before you begin to work with the stock. In the materials lists, we will specify pine unless a more consistently straight-grained wood such as fir is required or another species is used for aesthetic reasons. Feel free to substitute more rot-resistant or elegant species for pine wherever you choose.

With all that in mind, a quick thumb through this book will tell you what approach we suggest. Nearly all of the more complex designs are made from plywood, while the rustic and simple models are built of solid lumber. From a creative standpoint, when trying to build birdhouses that resemble human habitations but are livable for birds, there's nothing like plywood.

24

Complex Trim

Many of the more complex designs in this book use tiny detail pieces of wood. Some of these can be purchased as preformed pieces at doll house and craft supply stores. Otherwise, lattice and outside corner molding—available at any lumberyard—will either suffice or at least provide stock for preparing the finished pieces. Lattice is typically available in 1/4" X 1-1/2" size, though some yards stock other widths. Most suppliers carry both 1/4" X 3/4" and 1/4" X 1-1/16" outside corner. Both lumberyards and hardware stores carry the hardwood dowel used for perches on the houses which have them.

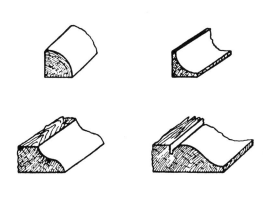

Fasteners

Use only corrosion-resistant metal parts in your birdhouse. Screws and nails should be galvanized (either hot-dipped or electrogalvanized) steel, brass, or stainless steel. Just about any hardware store will carry galvanized nails and screws; brass screws are usually sold as specialty items in a compartmented case; few hardware stores carry stainless steel fasteners, but they can be ordered through the mail. Any exposed hinges, latches, or catches should be solid, not plated, stainless or brass. The yellow plating on most standard-duty fittings oxidizes quickly and makes an unsightly mess, streaking adjacent wood black. A well-stocked hardware store will have them; otherwise, you'll have to order them through the mail.

Adhesives

Some glues are easy to apply; some are strong; others are inexpensive; still others are waterproof. None is all four. With that sobering news up front, consider using hot-melt glue to build your birdhouse. If you don't already have a hot-melt glue gun, you'll have to buy one and a supply of white (not amber) glue "cartridges" to load into its breech. Further, don't substitute hot-melt glue for adequate fasteners. It's a relatively low-strength adhesive. Nonetheless, hot-melt glue does have three significant advantages: 1) it's virtually waterproof, 2) it will fill in gaps in joinery, sealing the house, and 3) as long as you're quick—it sets in 20 to 30 seconds—it's very easy to use, requiring no clamping.

What are some other choices for sticking? Two-part resorcinol is the strongest, most waterproof of wood-to-wood adhesives. Counter those qualities with mixing, an ugly dried-blood color, a displeasing odor, a 24-hour curing time that requires clamping, and a minimum expenditure of about $15. Two-part epoxy can fill gaps just as well as hot-melt glue, and the better grades are very waterproof. To counter those qualities, epoxy is very expensive and has a short "pot life" (the time after mixing that it remains usable). Plain old carpenter's glue (called yellow or aliphatic resin) has little water resistance but will prove adequate in areas protected from weather.

FLATHEAD WOOD SCREWS

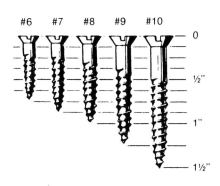

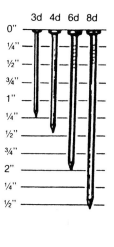

Finishes

You might be surprised to learn that the primary purpose of finish on wood is not to protect the surface from deterioration. Left to the elements, most woods only weather at a rate of about 1/4" per century. Wood gets coated more for structural and aesthetic reasons than to protect it from weathering.

Unsealed wood exchanges moisture readily with the atmosphere. When relative humidity is high, the wood adsorbs water and expands; when the air dries, the wood loses water and shrinks. In many climates, relative humidity changes significantly on a seasonal or even daily basis, stressing the joints of a wooden assemblage and the fibers themselves. Furthermore, stresses between different sections of an uncoated wooden structure can develop when the sun shines on one side and not on the other. Heat will drive surface water from rain or dew into the wood on the sunny side, expanding the material in only one part of the birdhouse.

Still, structural concerns don't demand that all wood be finished. Every birdhouse in this book is substantial enough to withstand wood movement caused by the average climate's wetting and drying cycles. Thus, your taste in finishes, or your love of a natural weathered appearance, can rule.

A completely unfinished birdhouse can be very attractive—from the day you put it out to years later as its appearance matures. Because the house will change over the years, you'll have the opportunity to participate in a small way in a natural process. And, there's a good chance that your tenants will prefer this minimalist approach. If you do decide to leave your birdhouse unfinished, don't be surprised when the exposed wood changes color. In general, the surface will turn some shade of gray, turning lighter in the cast of dark woods and darker in the case of light woods.

Certain general guidelines pertain to any finish you apply to a birdhouse. First, apply the finish to all sides of each piece of wood. Wood with just one or a few sealed surfaces may warp more than completely uncoated wood. Pay particular attention to end grain, since it absorbs much more finish than face grain. Plywood needs to have all edges thoroughly sealed or it will be prone to delaminate. Depending on the type of joints your house has, you may have to seal the wood before assembling the house to ensure equal coverage.

Among the clear coatings, marine spar varnish is one of the most durable and forms the best seal when applied in one or two coats. Polyurethane varnish rated for sunlight exposure also works well but may require three coats for a good seal. Penetrating finishes are also very appealing, in part because they're so easy to apply. Danish oil stands up well to the outdoors, as long as it's reapplied every year or two. And tung oil is gaining favor with many woodworkers as an outdoor finish. No penetrating finish seals as thoroughly as a thick surface finish, but they seem to reduce wood movement by their very nature.

About Dimensions

Any exterior-rated paint, alkyd or latex, will work well on a birdhouse, but we recommend that you look for one that does not contain mercury. Intended as a fungicide, this toxic chemical has been implicated recently in health problems experienced by people applying paints containing it. Paints with mercury may not be good for you or our feathered friends. Another thing to look for in a paint is its ultraviolet resistance. Most paint advertisements make more of the ability to cover in one coat, which is no great concern on a small project. Assurances about longevity might be more valuable.

That said, most veteran painters still maintain that oil-based paints last longer outdoors than the water-based latex varieties, while many building scientists claim that latex's flexibility makes it more durable in a harsh environment. Suffice to say that the debate between oil and water advocates is a heated one; they simply don't mix.

When you're considering colors to paint a birdhouse, bear in mind that the aesthetic preferences of birds and people differ considerably. Not surprisingly, most birds prefer natural or tan finishes, though purple martins are pleased by white, too. Several of the birdhouses in this book are decorated more to suit humans than birds.

Whatever coating you put on your birdhouse, don't place the dwelling out for occupancy as soon as it's dry. All finishes contain volatile compounds that allow them to be spread as a liquid and then thicken or dry. The odor of these evaporating chemicals is unpleasant (or even hazardous) for birds and humans. After finishing, let your birdhouse air in your wood shop or outdoors for at least two weeks, or until there's no perceptible odor.

For consistency, we've adopted some standard ways of noting sizes in this book. First, we steered clear of the metric system, since inches still seem to hold sway in woodworking. For you metric converts, see the chart on page 128 for standard conversions.

As you may know, lumber in the U.S. isn't always what it says it is. When a board is called a 1x (one-by), it's not actually an inch thick (actually more or less 3/4", depending). In the text and materials list, none of these nominal dimensions carry inch (") marks. So, now when you see a *naked* number, you know what's up. On the other hand, plywood and other manufactured lumber is pretty darn close to its retail description. For our purposes, we can consider 3/4" plywood to be just that.

About the Materials Lists

All the major materials used in building a bird house are listed in the order that they're needed, with the exception that fasteners are all saved for the end. The exact dimensions of a finished component are not necessarily listed; rather, the stock needed to prepare the part is listed. In some cases that will be the finished piece; in others, such as a mitered gable end, it will not. As noted previously, the types of materials should be considered as generic suggestions. For example, many lumber components are listed as "pine." You should certainly feel free to substitute a better material or one that's more readily available in your area. We listed other materials only when we considered the choice to be particularly important.

MATERIALS LIST

1 x 12 x 23" Pine
(2) 1 x 6" x 9-1/2" Pine
1 x 9-1/2" x 18" Pine
(2) 1 x 7-1/2" x 9-3/4" Pine
(2) 1 x 6" x 12-5/8" Pine
(2) 1 x 7" x 10" Pine
(20) no.8 x 1-1/2" Brass flathead woodscrews

Tools and Techniques

Special Tools

Most of the birdhouses described in this book are easy woodworking projects, and even the more complex houses involve only greater detail work. Don't be intimidated because your workshop and skills may fall a little short of cabinetmaker class. Small-scale projects such as these are a great way to gain experience without making major expenditures, and we'll help to point out potential pitfalls. For the more accomplished craftsperson, we hope you'll use these designs as springboards for more daring projects—expressions of your own creativity.

Few of the projects in this book require exotic tools. In fact, most go together easily with nothing more than a saw, a drill (and appropriate bits), a hammer, and a screwdriver. In many instances, however, access to a tablesaw will save time and likely improve the finished product. This stationary tool is particularly helpful for cutting accurate bevels and miters and forming lap joints. A combination blade with carbide-tipped teeth (40 of them for a 10" model) should make smooth crosscuts in lumber and easily handle the light ripping in these projects. In nearly all cases, where a dado is involved we've simply clamped more than one standard blade into the tablesaw to achieve multiples of the standard 1/8" kerf. If you use plywood for your project, you'll definitely want to cut it with a power circular saw or a tablesaw, either of which can hold a panel-cutting blade for smooth cuts. All but the finest-toothed handsaws will splinter plywood veneer. Should any project require more powerful weaponry that mentioned here, we'll give you fair warning.

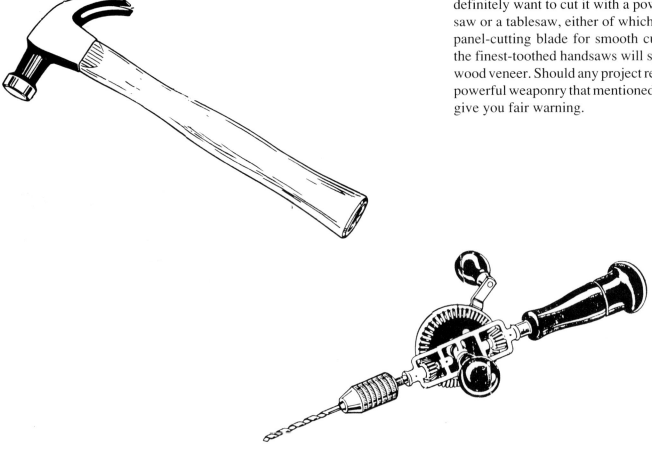

Construction Tips

PLYWOOD: As easy as it is to work with, plywood imposes one important requirement on the birdhouse builder: every edge exposes wood end grain, which must be protected from water. Extra coats of paint will be needed here, or the cut edge should be butted against another piece of wood (perhaps a piece of molding, as detailed later) and sealed with caulk.

Good gluing technique is particularly important with plywood, since nails and screws do not find very firm footing in the end grain, with its laminations. (Think of nails, in particular, as little more than clamps to hold the pieces in place while the glue sets.) Though glues are very strong, they are not designed to fill gaps. Thus, a solid glue joint should have little space between the joined pieces. For that reason, cuts need to be square and smooth, and the pieces should be held together tightly while the adhesive cures.

There is little point in using screws in plywood end grain, unless they're needed to make a part removable. Holes would have to be drilled for them to prevent the laminations from separating, and they would have little holding power anyway. Stick to good gluing technique and nails.

Should you adapt a design or develop one of your own that includes small, square holes, you'll find them a challenge to cut in plywood. A sabre saw with a fine-toothed blade is the best tool, but you can get by with an inexpensive coping saw and a bit of technique. When cutting the outer veneers of the plywood, hold the blade at about a 45° angle to the surface to avoid splitting the veneer and pulling it away from the surface. If you install the blade in the saw so that it cuts on the pull stroke, the crucial cut will be easy to see, rather than being hidden below the work. To keep the cut square and straight, don't force the blade forward, let it draw itself into the material.

LUMBER: There's very little to say about sawing boards that hasn't already been said elsewhere and that can't be learned more quickly by simply doing it. However, a few words about orientation might be helpful. If possible, on any design that has a platform that may pool water, arrange the walls of the house so the end grain is vertical—not butting up against the platform where water can wick up. Furthermore, if you care to go to the trouble to miter those vertical joints in the wall, you'll be rewarded with a tidier looking project that will last longer. Bear in mind, though, that mitered joints depend more on good gluing than do butt joints. They trade more surface area for less purchase for fasteners. Screws offer somewhat more strength than nails, but are handicapped when their threads have only end grain to grab hold of. Many woodworkers now use drywall screws for woodworking, because they can be driven without drilling and countersinking. If you decide to go this route, be sure to use corrosion-resistant screws—those designed for decks work well—to prevent unsightly oxidation stains.

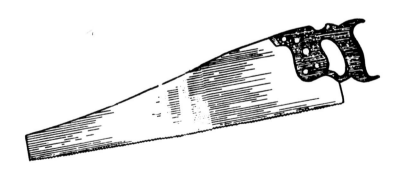

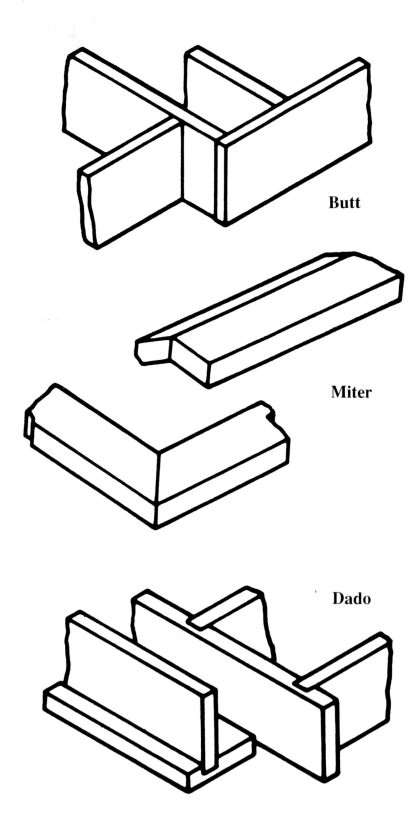

Butt

Miter

Dado

JOINERY: This isn't the place for a treatise on joints, but a brief review of terminology may help you wade through the construction explanations that follow. Basically, you'll only run into three types of joints here, all of them simple: butt, miter, and dado. A butt joint is where one square end of a piece of wood runs into the face or end of another. The weakest of all joints, it is still perfectly adequate when properly glued and nailed and supported by other intersecting boards. Mitered joints have two angled boards butting together. They're usually used to form a 90° corner, where appearance and protection of the end grain is important. Dado joints come in a variety of flavors, but most of the ones in this book are cross laps. A groove is cut in each board and the two grooves are meshed to cross the boards. This one's used for compartments in martin houses, for example.

SAFETY: It goes without saying that all power tools are potentially hazardous. In some instances, though, the small trim pieces in these bird houses require that you operate in particularly close proximity to the saw blade. You should be familiar with and use safety techniques such as push sticks, jigs, and feather sticks.

Always wear eye protection and a dust mask when working wood. Plus, if you're working with an aromatic species such as cedar, you may find that you need a respirator to stop vapors.

In the end, though, safety always depends most on common sense. If you're not sure, don't try it. If you're tired, stop.

Basic Designs & Details

Roughly speaking, all the designs in this book can be divided into three categories: platform, recessed floor, and multi-compartment (which can be either of the previous). Most of the platform houses will be mounted on poles, while the recessed floor models can be hung or mounted through their backs either to a pole or a building.

As we suggested a ways back, you might be better off avoiding platform designs if you live in a wet climate. Despite all your efforts to prevent water from pooling, the platform and its joint to the walls will get wet, and they will rot eventually.

You'll also want to note whether a particular design is suited to species common to your area. You desert rats, for example, probably won't find much purpose in building the Postmodern wood duck house. Likewise, the pileated woodpecker is somewhat limited in its range. Most of the other houses, however, should find tenants almost anywhere in the U.S.. Nesting species in the British Isles are more limited, but there's still ample opportunity to develop a backyard aviary.

Design possibilities are limitless, as these sketches begin to illustrate.

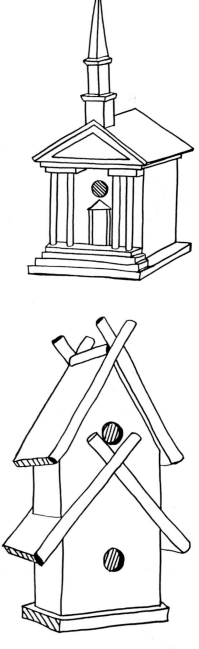

Roofs

The designs in this book are probably distinguished as much by roof type as they are by basic shape. We've got simple sheds, gables, hips, a mansard, pyramids (four and six sided), and even a gambrel barn. Since the roof is so fundamental to weather protection, it's worth spending a few minutes discussing materials and methods.

A rule of thumb is that the steeper the roof, the less you have to worry about it. As an extreme example, the chalet is all roof—and a steep one at that. For it, the painted plywood is perfectly adequate. A bit of caulk along the ridge protects the end grain of the plywood. At the other end of the spectrum, the spanish villa has a flat roof that demands the protection of an impervious coating.

Many of our houses have copper roofs, both because of its beauty and because it's so durable. Check with local sheet metal shops to find this material. If you're feeling at all adventuresome, you likely can bend up your own roofs. Copper bends easily over the corner of a table and is very forgiving. Once you see the layout, as shown here, a pyramid of copper is simple to cut out and form in a variety of sizes.

Ideally, the seams in a copper roof ought to be soldered. We recommend using an iron rather than a torch, since the latter will discolor the copper much more from heat. Soldering is much easier than it's stacked up to be. One basic rule will guide you: solder always flows toward heat—even uphill. Another important note on copper: always use copper fasteners to attach the roof the house; dissimilar materials will produce a reaction that will cause deterioration.

Elsewhere in the book we've used roll roofing, doll house shingles, raw cedar, and even auto body putty to protect our bird houses. Please don't view these as the only options. Use your imagination and the materials you know to go your own way.

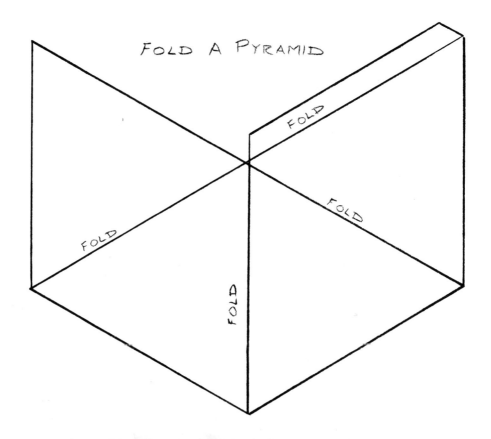

FOLD A PYRAMID

Cleanout

Every bird house should have some easy way to gain access for cleaning. Since the house will probably only be occupied for a few months each year, you'll want to remove old nesting materials and mess, and sanitize the interior after your tenants have taken flight. Different houses lend themselves to different cleanout approaches. Some of the simpler boxes can have removable sides, while the designs with a lot of detail on the facade may better have a removable roof. Another good approach is to have a removable floor, held in with pins or screws.

Multi-compartment units will require particular ingenuity. Roof access is surely the simplest approach to single-story designs. Multi-story designs may work better with a removable wall.

Ventilation and Drains

Every house also needs ventilation and drainage. In most cases, vents should be arranged under the roof eaves; slots or a series of 1/4" to 1/2" holes are better than one big hole, which will be more prone to leak wind-driven rain. Drain holes should be about 1/8" in diameter located in each corner.

Entry Hole

This may be the most crucial part of the bird house from the bird's point of view. If it's too large, unwanted intruders will take over. If it's too high, the occupants will have a hard time coming and going. If it's too low, they'll suffer in the weather.

Use either a hole saw or a spade bit to drill through a solid lumber bird house. Only the hole saw will produce satisfactory results with plywood. (Tip: If you file down the inner portions of a spade bit slightly, the tips will cut more cleaning when entering the material.) Any electrical drill with a 3/8" chuck can handle these bits, but expect the job to take a while longer with a light-duty drill.

Once you've drilled the opening, bore another hole of the same size in a scrap piece of 3/4"-thick stock. Then glue this to the inside of the wall to extend the depth of the hole inward. Once the glue sets, roughen the inside surface of the opening with a rasp file to give bird claws something to hold on to.

Wood duck houses also need a ladder to help the ducklings come and go. One simple solution is to tack or staple some chicken wire to a length of 2"-wide lattice. The ladder runs from the inside of the hole down to the floor of the house.

The Nightingale

Functional bird houses can be sited imaginatively to enhance public places (opposite), or integrated as components of outdoor sculpture (above).

Mounting

Birds are much more likely to take up residence if your bird house is firmly mounted. As already mentioned, platform houses should go on poles. This could be a pressure treated 4 x 4 braced with L brackets or 2 x 4 triangles or even a section of 3" plastic plumbing pipe with a closet flange (used to connect toilets). In either case, sink the pole at least 18" with a post hole digger to provide stability. Wooden posts ought to have gravel at the bottom of the hole for drainage. Well-packed dirt around either type of pole should offer plenty of support; concrete isn't necessary.

To mount houses with recessed floors, either attach them to a tree, fence post, or wall, or run a post up the back. Of course, some of the larger houses are restricted in their mounting options. The Southern Mansion is heavy enough that it really needs wall mounting. And in some cases, the mounting actually becomes a part of the design.

Whatever approach you take to mounting the house, be sure it's set at the right height and in a habitat suitable to the species. Check back to the House-Nesting Birds chart (pages 16 & 17) for pointers. You can further encourage occupancy by orienting the entry hole toward the sun and away from any prevailing wind-driven rain. Further, as much as we like to watch them come and go, timid birds are more likely to move in if the entry faces away from people. That means keeping bird houses and feeders away from heavy traffic areas such as driveways and sidewalks. You may also find that birds prefer locations at the edge of woods or fields—border habitat—where there are few obstructions for approach and departure.

Predator Barriers

In the chapter, Unwanted Guests, we discussed in some detail the problem of various predators. Beyond the techniques mentioned there, you can install physical barriers that will discourage, if not eliminate, the acting out of instincts.

The most common barrier is a simple cone about 18" in diameter that wraps around the pole that supports the house or feeder. You can fashion one from aluminum sheet (thinner is better, as long as it will hold shape in the wind), as shown in the accompanying illustration. Assemble and mount the cone with self-tapping sheet metal screws. Your local hardware store will have these, as well as a bit for your electric drill to drive them. Be sure to place it far enough up the pole that pests can't leap right over it from the ground.

A cone barrier will probably discourage cats, but we've watched many a squirrel perform miraculous climbing feats to surmount them. If squirrels are a problem with a feeder, probably your best bet is to hang it on a wire (they'll gnaw through rope) attached to another wire spanning two trees, or a tree and a building. Don't locate the feeder within 30' of a tree or building; squirrels can jump long distances.

Another way to foil cats is to fence the area beneath a feeder or spread chicken wire on the ground. Attempts to leap will be compromised by an inability to build up speed.

One final concern about feeders and predators: no matter how well protected a feeder may be, birds that feed on the ground are going to be vulnerable. Seed will spill, and birds will collect there. Cats will take their toll—fences and chicken wire not withstanding. Try to reduce the amount of seed that spills by using a platform, and do your best to keep pets at bay. You may find, however, that the only way to end the carnage is to get rid of the feeder.

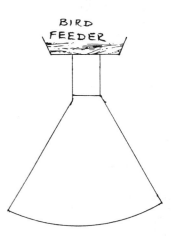

The Golden Oriole

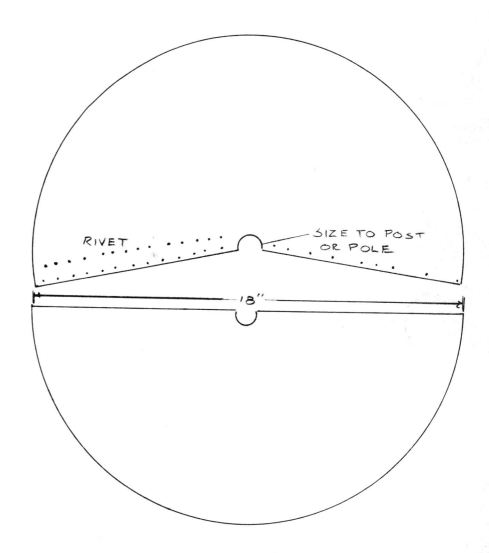

The BIRD HOUSES

Gourds

If you've been wondering what good gourds are, ask a purple martin. Now that we've invented synthetic bowls and cups, gourds are seldom used for much other than ornamentation. That's a shame, because they offer ideal bird quarters.

There's little to say about building a gourd bird house. Just drill an appropriate-size hole with a hole saw. But there's a bit more to say about the creative possibilities of Nature's own bird house.

Gourds invite decoration—Southwestern pueblo, as we chose, or even more natural motifs. But there's more.

Gourds grow readily anywhere pumpkins and squash thrive. Consider planting your own suburb. They like a deep, well-drained soil (not too much fertilizer; they'll over-produce foliage). Gourds can actually be molded as they're grown. With careful bending by hand or with tape, you may find a pink flamingo and other exotics hiding in your garden.

The Titmouse

Gourd houses are easily hung in trees, and prove to be quite attractive when painted.

Split-Log House

When you've had your fill of the confines of the workshop and the precision of cabinetmaking, you might enjoy woodworking on a cruder scale. Crank up the chainsaw, head for the woods, and get back to basics.

Find a straight-grained log about 8" diameter, and cut a 12" cross-section—with one end square and the other on a slant. Next, rip about a 2" slab off square to the sloping end, removing the longer side. This cut needs to be as square and flat as possible. (The trick here is to keep the log from moving while you saw; wedge it between other logs. Also, you'll probably have better luck if you keep the angle of the bar to the length of the log small. The saw will cut better, and more of the bar will be in the wood, helping keep the cut straight.)

With that done, remove 2" from each end, making the cuts as square and clean as you're able. (If you have a band saw, use it!) Save these two cutoffs. The sloping end will be reattached as the roof, and the square one will become the floor.

Now it's time to remove a 4" wide, 4" deep chamber from the heart of the log. Set the 8" section flat, with its rounded side down, and make five 4"-deep incisions lengthwise and about an inch apart in the flat face. Then put the chainsaw away, and get comfortable with a large (at least 1") chisel and a mallet. (Here's where you find out how good you are at judging straight grain from the outside.) Work your way down with the chisel through the 1" sections left by the saw cuts until you've hollowed out a 4"-deep, 4"-wide chamber.

Use a 1-1/4" (for house wrens) or 1-1/2" (for Bewick's, Carolina, and other wrens) bit to bore a hole into the middle of the chamber. Then, at your option, bore a smaller hole below to insert a piece of dowel for a perch.

All that's left is to reattach the top and bottom (drilling lead holes for 16d galvanized nails so the wood won't split). If you did a tidy job removing them, the cut lines shouldn't be very obvious.

The house could either be attached directly to a tree, to close up the back, or you could add a board to the back to seal the chamber. The latter approach gives you more mounting options, but the house is really at its best in full camouflage.

The Three-Toed Woodpecker

Sawmill leavings make great raw material for avian contractors. You may have seen bird houses and feeders resembling these before, and wondered where the builders got those lovely boards with the bark left on. Answer: by the ton from a sawmill. When the board factory squares up a log, slabs are left—useful only to wood burners, and the artisan with an eye for found materials.

Picky Bird Panacea

Rustic houses are particularly well-suited to species that are picky about the spaces they'll inhabit. You may have better luck attracting woodpeckers and wood ducks, for example, if you build them a bark-faced or log house of suitable dimensions.

Construction

Should you have a source for bark-on slabs, you ought to try working with them. The single flat surface doesn't lend itself to the conventional geometry of woodworking but leaves many opportunities for inventive techniques.

A few guidelines: the most popular bark-faced slabs are birch (in the northeast), poplar (in the southeast), and pine (elsewhere). They are readily available, and the birch has a particularly attractive bark. As the layer of wood right below the bark (the sapwood) in these species dries, it will shrink and tend to pull away from the bark. If you drive your nails through the bark and into the solid wood, things will hang together better down the road. Wherever possible, try to give the end grain a little protection by covering it with small branches.

Other than that, these dwellings ought to be free-form art. Let the materials inspire you which direction to go.

To create the twig-faced house, start with a basic box—even a store-bought item will serve admirably. Then visit your backyard or a nearby field to select your building materials. Look for straight bushes, water shoots, grasses, vines, and other colorful vegetation that is dry and has firmly attached bark (or, remove the bark). In any regrown section of disturbed ground, you should be able to find a vivid selection of browns, greens, yellows, and even reds among the underbrush.

Back at home, arm yourself with a hot-melt glue gun, a small hand saw, a utility knife, and pruning shears, and begin cutting and attaching twigs to the front of the house. Remember that the lengths of wood should overlap the ones that will be attached to the sides. Leave extra length, which can be trimmed later.

Our house capitalizes on subtle geometric patterns accentuated by color changes, all of which is visually broken by the twist of red-berried vine around the hole. On the roof are dried grasses held in place by lengths of wisteria attached to the top with 4d galvanized nails. The options are, of course, as boundless as your sources and your imagination.

Old Crows' Tavern

If you wanted a vintage bottle of wine, would you buy this year's pickings and wait? Of course not. Likewise here, where the builders sought the appearance of an aging—should we say moldering?—backroad watering hole.

And what better source of that look could there be than old building materials? Faced with sections of driftwood board and capped with old sheet metal, this is actually a conventional wooden bird house beneath. The interior dimensions of that inner box and the diameter of the entry hole could be set to suit a number of smaller nesting birds, though this example is best suited to wrens or chickadees.

Barn wood may be the most readily available material for building new old bird houses. The more weathered and cracked, the better. A few tips, though: watch out for nails, which are hard to spot when rusted but still perfectly capable of ruining a saw; use a coarse rip blade to leave saw marks on the wood for authenticity; and plan on ending up with a dull saw blade, as old wood gets very hard.

Proper painting is just as important as the material it's applied to. Try thinning flat white paint and rubbing it on with a cloth or sponge. Use a dry cloth to smudge off corners to achieve a worn look. Black paint can be used in a similar way to good effect on the roof and for windows.

As is the case with nearly every project in this book, the point is inspiration, not imitation. Scrounge around to see what you can find. Why, even the nails could be recycled.

The Crow

Log Cabin

MATERIALS LIST

(2) 1 x 8 x 8-3/4" Pine
(2) 1 x 3" x 7" Pine
(4) 3/4" x 4' Dowels
3/4" x 3' Dowels
3/8" x 2" x 3" Plywood
(2) 3/8 x 1" x 3" Plywood
1 x 3/4" x 4" Pine
1 x 8 x 7" Pine
(2) 1 x 8 x 11" Pine
1 x 2 x 2-1/2" Pine
1/4" x 1" Dowels
6d Galvanized finish nails
8d Galvanized finish nails
(4) 3/16" x 4" steel rods

Toy Houses

Another attractive and entertaining approach to building log bird houses is to use one of the many toy construction sets, fitting the pieces with glue and small nails for permanence. You could end up with positively presidential accommodations.

To tell the truth, this pioneering approach to bird lodgings is a log house in appearance only. Much simpler to construct than some twig amalgam, our pine box achieves the traditional look with a facade fashioned of halved 3/4" dowels, while retaining the virtues of solid lumber's strength and weather-resistance. Not only is it fun to look at, you'll also be entertained by this project's uncanny use of materials.

Start by sawing the 8-3/4"-long front and back walls from 1 x 8 stock. Then connect points 4" up each 7-1/4" side with one in the center of the 8-3/4" top. Create the roof peak by sawing along these lines (the angle is about 37°). Don't bother with the entry hole at this point; you can drill it after the log siding is in place. The side walls are only 3" high, to leave

a 1" ventilation space between their tops and the roof. You can get both of these from one 7"-long piece of 1 x 8 by ripping the board twice. The leftovers will prove useful later.

You'll need four 4' lengths and part of another 3' length of 3/4" dowel for the logs. Go ahead and rip all these in half on the tablesaw. The accompanying cutting chart and diagram give you the dimensions of the various logs. The specified lengths allow for final trimming to square up the ends and to miter to the correct angle. Note also that the logs on the front and back and below the roofline will overhang to be flush with the side logs.

Before siding the house, cut out the 2" x 3" door and the two 1-1/4" x 2" windows from 3/8" plywood and the 1 x 3/4" x 4" door awning from that scrap of 1 x 8 left from the side walls. Beveling the overhang to 30° or so is a nice touch. Nail and glue these parts in place at the following locations: the front door

2" from the left wall, the overhang 1-3/4" from the left wall and flush to the top of the door, and the windows 1-3/4" from an end. (We alternated ours front and back.)

Now apply the siding, butting the pieces snugly against the door, overhang, and windows. (Be careful not to put any nails where the entry hole will be.) With that done, run the walls through the tablesaw, inside down, to square up the ends of the logs. Test fit the front and back walls to the sides to get the overlap just right. Then set the miter gauge to the roof slope angle and trim all the upper logs flush with the front and back walls. At this point, you can also drill the 1-1/2" entry hole centered 2-1/2" below the roof peak.

Assemble the walls of the house with 8d galvanized finish nails; drilling lead holes here will help avoid having deviant nails emerge from the walls.

The base of the house is 1 x 8 x 7", trimmed to fit loosely between the walls. Rather than being nailed in place, it's held by four removable 3/16" x 4" bent steel rods, to offer access for cleaning. Set the house on its side with the floor in place, and bore the 3/16" holes for the rods through the side walls and into the base.

Two 11" pieces of 1 x 8, with one edge beveled to match the roof slope (about 37°), make up the roof. Nail these to the tops of the front and back walls and to the central ridge beam made from a 7" length of scrap. A bead of silicone caulk will help seal the roof's peak.

The finishing touch is the chimney, made of a piece of 1 x 2 about 2-1/2" long. For authentic stovepipe, add an inch of 1/4" dowel to the top of that.

Dark stain helps the birch dowels better resemble bark-on logs, and a coating of water sealer will prevent the wood from graying so quickly. Neighbors will be none the wiser, and your feathered friends won't say a word.

The Mountain Finch

Log Facade Cutting Chart

Code	Qty.	Size
A	4	2-1/2"
B	4	5-1/4"
C	1	2-1/4"
D	1	3-1/2"
E	7	9-3/4"
F	2	7"
G	2	5"
H	2	3"
I	2	1"
J	2	8-3/4"
K	6	2"
L	6	5-3/4"
M	2	1-1/4"

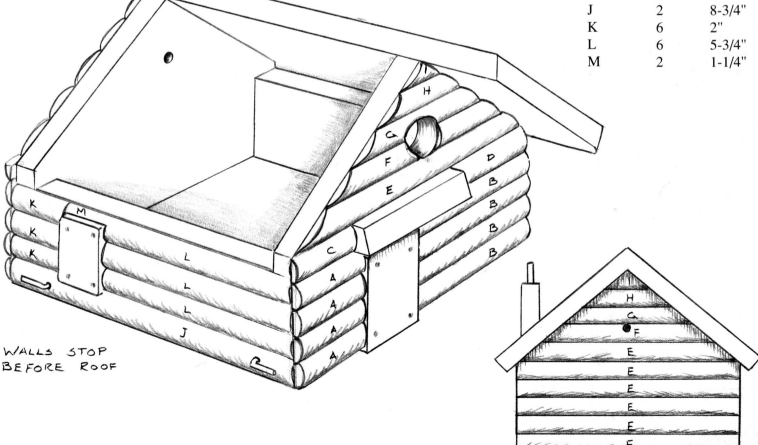

WALLS STOP BEFORE ROOF

Barn Owl Barn

MATERIALS LIST

- (2) 1 X 10-5/8" X 20" Western red cedar
- (2) 1 X 8-1/2" X 20" Western red cedar
- (4) 1 X 8 X 22" Beveled, notch-lap siding
- 2 X 2 X 22-5/8" Western red cedar
- (2) 1/2" x 3/4" x 7" Western red cedar
- (3) 1/2" x 3/4" x 3-1/2" Western red cedar
- (4) 1/2" x 3/4" x 4" Western red cedar
- (10) no.8 x 1-1/4" Brass flathead woodscrews
- (4) Button screw hole plugs
- 8d Galvanized finish nails
- 6d Galvanized finish nails
- 4d Galvanized finish nails

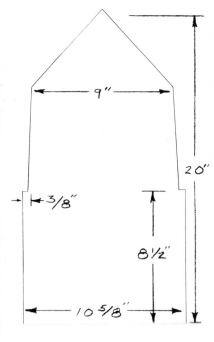

A barn owl's nesting needs are unique, precluding this house's use by other common species. No matter. To our way of thinking, the exhilaration of discovering this silent predator overhead, faintly silhouetted against the night sky, is worth every effort to offer suitable habitat.

Fittingly enough, the construction techniques used in the Owl Barn are unique among this collection. Nearly all its parts are from western red cedar, some of them plain boards and others of beveled, notch-lap siding. Start by cutting out the front and back walls from 1 x 12, using the accompanying cutting diagram. It's important to follow the dimensions closely, so the siding will fit snugly. Once that's done, bore the 6" hole (or cut it out with a saber or coping saw) 5" on center above the base.

Next, rip a piece of 1 x 12 that's 20-1/8" long down to 8-1/2" width. Then, cut the board exactly in half to form the two walls. To simulate barn siding, we cut 1/16"-deep saw kerfs every 1-1/4" along these boards. Countersink no.8 x 1-1/4" brass flathead woodscrews through the sides and into the edges of the front and back walls. Cover the screws with button screw hole plugs.

The roof of the house consists for four 22" pieces of 1 x 8 beveled, notch-lap siding. Overlap these boards an equal amount front and rear, and nail them to the walls with 6d galvanized finish nails. To cover the roof peak, cut a 22-5/8" piece of 2 x 2. Next, tilt the tablesaw blade to 45° and set the rip fence so it's 1/4" from the base of the blade. Run the 2 x 2 through in both directions to bevel its sides. Next, set the blade height to 1/2" and move the rip fence in so that it's 1/8" from the base of the blade. Create a W notch in the 2 x 2 by pushing it through twice. The remaining stock in the center of the notch fits into the gap between the roof boards. Miter each end of this board about 30°, and secure it to the roof peak by nailing it from the underside.

Prepare the base by ripping an 18-1/2"-long piece of 3/4" cedar down to a width of 10-5/8". Drill 1/4" drain holes in the corners and center of this floor, and secure the board with screws countersunk through the walls and into the edge of the floor.

All the decorative trim is formed from 1/2" x 3/4" stock. Prepare about 4' of this material by ripping strips from the edge of a piece of 1x cedar. To trim the entry hole to look like a barn door, set your miter gauge to 22-1/2°, and cut two 7" pieces mitered on one end and three 3-1/2" pieces mitered on both ends. For the loft, reset the miter gauge to 45°, and cut four 4" strips mitered at both ends.

Black was the unquestioned choice for coloring the roof, but we have to admit to being torn about painting the cedar walls. The red works well—perhaps counterpointed by a white billboard on the roof?—but the walls might also have been effective left natural. In any event, the white trim offers worthwhile visual relief. The decorative wagon wheel came from a shopping spree in the doll house section at a local craft store. Likewise, model railroad shops offer a variety of knickknacks that can enhance a fanciful bird house.

The Female Short-Eared Owl

The Little House Out Back

Here's a one-holer of a different sort. Although not as ornate (or imposing!) as some of our nest boxes, this little shelter, modeled after the standard rural backyard convenience, is both eminently practical—since it can be sized to suit many of the smaller house-nesting bird species—and loaded with enough boondocks charm to serve as an indoor conversation piece, complementing any country decor.

Its construction is far from difficult, too. The entire house is cut from 1x pine and held together with 6d galvanized finish nails.

Begin by shaping the two sides of the roof. First cut a 1 x 6 to a length of 15-1/8" (a blade width longer than two roof sides). Then set your table saw blade to 30°, and rip one edge of the board to establish the peak bevel. Crosscut this board exactly in the middle, and you'll end up with two 1 x 6 x 7-1/2" roof boards. To support the roof peak from the under side and offer additional weather protection, cut two 30° bevels to form a 60° edge on a piece of 1x scrap about 5-3/8" long. A second length of 1x scrap, ripped to 1" thickness, can be sawn to length to form the angled perch.

Working downward, miter one end of each 1 x 4" x 10" front and back board to form the 60° peak. In one of these, bore the 1-1/4" diameter entry hole 1-3/4" on center below the peak. (You can later paint the tell-tale crescent moon in black as we've done. Or, as an alternative, use a jig-saw to cut out a moon large enough to contain the hole desired; then back that crescent with a black-painted scrap of 1/4" plywood in which the actual entry hole has been bored.) The back ought to have a 1/4" hole for mounting. The perch, which you cut in the previous paragraph, is nailed an inch below the hole at about a 30° angle.

The sides of the house are each 1 x 6 x 8-1/2", with the tops beveled at 30° to parallel the roof. Align the bases of these walls with the bases of the front and back; the gap between the top of the wall and the roof is left for ventilation.

With that done, simply cut out the oversized 1 x 6 x 7-1/2" base and the 1 x 3-15/16" x 3-15/16" base plug, which measures slightly smaller than the interior of the finished bird house. (Remember, if this fit is too snug, warpage will make the base difficult to remove for cleaning.) Nail these two parts together, centering the square in the width and positioning it 1-1/4" from the back of the base. Then drill 1/4" drainage holes.

Use a rasp and/or sandpaper to smooth any sharp corners, and assemble the bird house, securing each joint with glue and nails. Overlap the roof boards 1/2" to the rear, so the front receives the most weather protection. Then fit the base piece into the structure, and drill 1/4" holes toward the front of the right side and the rear of the left side, close enough to the bottom to allow the bit to go cleanly through the wall and into the interior base. Use a vise to bend two short pieces of 3/16" steel rod, which will hold the whole assembly together until it's time for spring cleaning.

It's our feeling that the outhouse should have a rustic look. So, other than painting the moon, you might limit your brush work to the application of a clear sealant on the rest of the structure, hoping it'll achieve a weathered look in time. Further authenticity might be added by covering the peak with a glued-on scrap of asphalt roofing paper.

Finally, mount the little house where you can keep an eye on it. Once your guests have taken up residence, you'll want to be "privy" to their comings and goings.

The Nuthatch

MATERIALS LIST

(2) 1 x 6 x 7-1/2" Pine
(2) 1 x 4" x 10" Pine
1 x 1" x 3" Pine
(2) 1 x 6 x 8-1/2" Pine
1 x 6 x 7-1/2" Pine
1 x 3-15/16" x 3-15/16" Pine
3/16" Steel rod
6d Galvanized finish nails

MATERIALS LIST

(2) 1 x 7-1/4" x 9" Pine
(2) 1 x 6 x 7" Pine
1 x 1" x 3" Pine
(2) 1 x 4-1/2" x 4-1/2" Pine
1 x 4-1/4" x 7-3/4" Pine
1 x 2" x 4-7/16" Pine
6d Galvanized finish nails
no.8 x 1-1/2" Brass flathead
   woodscrews

It's amazing how a few simple changes in shape and decoration can take a bird house from the ridiculous to the sublime, transforming it from a backwoods commode into a post house at the guarded border of a mythical country.

Most of the procedures for building this bird house are the same as those used for the outhouse, the main difference being the sloped walls. Start with the 1 x 7-1/4" x 9" roof boards, sawing them from a 1 x 8 x 18-1/8" beveled at 30°. Again, an appropriately beveled piece of 1x ought to be cut to go beneath the peak for support and weather protection.

Next, miter 60° points in two 7" lengths of 1 x 6. Find the center of the base (2-3/4" from either edge) of one, mark points 1-13/16" on both sides of the center, and connect these points with outer edges of the roof peak bevels. Now, stacking the marked piece atop the other one with their square bases against the miter gauge, set the gauge to the appropriate angle (about 10°), cut, flop, and cut again. At this time, go ahead and bore the 1-1/4" entry hole centered 2-1/2" below the peak. The 1 x 1" x 3" perch can also be formed and nailed in place.

To bevel the bottoms of the sides, start with about 10 inches of 1 x 6" pine, set the tablesaw blade to the same angle used to profile the front and back, and rip the board to leave a 4-1/2" width. Return the blade to vertical and cut out two 4-1/2" pieces from this stock.

The 1 x 4-1/4" x 7-3/4" base of the guardhouse and its 1 x 2" x 4-7/16" interior floor can now be cut, remembering that the latter is sized to allow for a little warpage. Position the floor centered in the width of the base and 1-1/4" from the back, nail the two pieces together, and drill the 1/4" drainage holes in the assembly. With that done, use 6d galvanized finish nails and glue to assemble the guardhouse. Then insert the base and drill and countersink holes to accommodate the no.8 x 1-1/2" brass flathead wood screws that will hold everything together until you need to clean it out.

The Yellow Wren

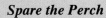

We choose a jaunty diagonally-striped paint scheme to make our guard post visible to weary travelers, but this basic bird house shape lends itself to many interpretations. For instance, with a 1" x 1" x 1" red chimney, dark roof, pastel walls and some painted-on windows, the guardhouse could be transformed into a country cottage. Whatever exterior decor you decide on, we're sure that you'll find each year's new flock of immigrants welcome additions to the population of your own backyard kingdom.

Spare the Perch

The color scheme of this house may be a bit off-putting to its intended tenants, wrens. To discourage sparrows—which have considerably less discriminating taste in housing—from taking over, omit the perch from this design.

54

Sky-Way Toll-Booth

Two-sided nesting platforms, preferred by robins and other claustrophobic species, are probably the simplest of bird houses. Still, as our toll-booth platform proves, even a basic design can come into its own with creative use of paints and accessories.

The platform itself couldn't be much easier to make. To begin, cut three rectangles from 1x lumber. The first, 8-1/8" x 9" will form the roof; the second, 8-1/8" x 12", the back; and the third, 7" x 8-1/8", the base. Next, cut a 6" x 9-1/2" rectangle, and miter one end at 45° to form a peak. (At this time you might also want to cut the 45° wedge from one of the short ends of the roof so it will fit flush with the wall and back.) Now use a jig saw, coping saw, or band saw to cut the scoop, as shown, from the front of the single wall. The roof, wall, back and floor can be assembled now, using no.8 x 1-1/4" brass flathead woodscrews and glue, or set aside for painting prior to final assembly.

The window consists of a 2" x 3" block of 1/2" plywood. The stop sign and barrier will probably call for jig-saw work; both are cut from 1/4" plywood (or any thin stock). The coin box has several parts. First, butt two 1x blocks, one 3/4" x 2-1/2" and the other 1-1/2" x 2-1/2". The spacers, which separate the two above blocks and leave room for the toll gate, are cut from 1/4" scrap. Make the first approximately 3/4" x 1-1/4" and the second about 1/2" x 3/4". The cap is a halved length of 3/4" dowel, cut to span the top of the block and spacer assembly.

At this point you should probably paint the various components with exterior grade alkyd or latex paint. We chose bright green and yellow for the nesting platform itself, silver for the coin box, and black and yellow stripes for the toll gate. You might want to personalize your platform by taking a spin on the nearest expressway and copying the color scheme used there. (A tip: If you don't feel up to painting the details on the stop sign, check your local hobby store. They'll probably have similar signs ready-made for model railroads.)

When the finish has dried, complete the assembly, using 4d galvanized finish nails and glue to trap the gate between the coin-box blocks and to fasten the half-dowel in place. Simply glue the stop sign and window on.

All that's left is to hang your toll booth in the nearest flight path. Chances are a platform-nesting bird family will be moved to stop, and that they'll pay an ample toll in the beauty and wonder they bring to your backyard.

MATERIALS LIST

1 x 8-1/8" x 9" Pine
1 x 8-1/8" x 12" Pine
1 x 7" x 8-1/8" Pine
1 x 6" x 9-1/2" Pine
1/2" x 2" x 3" Plywood
1 x 3/4" x 2-1/2" Pine
1 x 1-1/2" x 2-1/2" Pine
1/4" x 2" x 15" Plywood
1/4" x 3/4" x 1-1/4" Plywood
1/4" x 1/2" x 3/4" Plywood
3/4" Dowel
4d Galvanized finish nails

The Redbreast

Bill Telephone

It may not have the portability of the newest cellular phones, but we think that our rendition of "Ma Bill's" basic black unit will get a lot of use (especially during "beak" calling hours). Better still, it's fairly simply to construct (with most of the pieces fashioned from common 1x pine) and should be as appealing to birds hoping to phone home as it is to its builders.

The sides begin as 1 x 8 x 18" rectangles. From one long edge of each, cut away a strip measuring 1-1/4" x 13-1/4". Then miter the step produced by this cut at a 15° angle, and cut a matching miter on the narrow top end.

The front of the phone is a piece of 1 x 6 measuring 15-3/4" long, while the back is a 1 x 6 x 20". Both boards should have 15° bevel cuts on one end. The roof is simply a 7-1/4" length of 1 x 8, and will later be fastened to the back with cabinet hinges. At this time you can also drill the 1-1/2" entry hole, centered 2-1/2" from the top of the front panel.

A directory shelf juts forward over the mitered step. Cut from 1 x 8, it measures 3-3/4", and one long end is beveled to 15° to mount flush with the front panel. Below it, you'll want to install a false front consisting of a 1 x 6 x 3-5/8" board.

The bird house was designed with two bases: One, a false floor, is a 1 x 6 piece measuring 5-1/2" and will be mounted flush with the bottom of the walls; the real base can be moved up inside to determine the depth of the nesting chamber. It measures the same as the false base, and ours is positioned 6" up from the bottom of the phone. Each should be drilled with four 1/2" drainage holes.

Assemble the sides and front first, using glue and 6d galvanized finish nails. Then position the bases, secure them on three sides, and go on to add the back and false front.

The dial is cut from 1/4" plywood with a 4" hole saw. An entry hole, matching that in the front of the bird house, is centered on this disc,

and a ring of 1/2" holes complete the piece, which can be glued in place.

To make the mouthpiece, use a 2-1/2" hole saw to cut a disc from a scrap of 1x, and tap nails onto its upper surface to produce a perforated texture. Mount this to a 1-1/2" x 1-1/2" x 3" base, and secure it, at a jaunty angle, to the front of the phone with a drill, glue, and a short section of 3/8" dowel.

The earpiece is simply a 2" x 4" block cut from 2x stock, then rasped and sanded to a bell-shaped flare. The top is drilled to accept the glued-in cord (either old electrical wire or heavy black nylon cord), the other end of which is knotted through a hole in the side of the phone.

Once it's painted to your liking, hang it from a likely tree. Then set a chair on the porch, pour a cold drink, take the indoor phone off the hook, and enjoy a restful evening waiting for . . . what else? Bird calls!

MATERIALS LIST

(2) 1 x 8 x 18" Pine
1 x 6 x 15-3/4" Pine
1 x 8 x 7-1/4" Pine
1 x 8 x 3-3/4" Pine
1 x 6 x 3-5/8" Pine
1 x 6 x 5-1/2" Pine
1/4" x 4" x 4" Plywood
1-1/2" x 1-1/2" x 3" Pine
3/8" x 3" Dowel
2 x 2" x 4" Pine
Black cord

The Jay

The Red Caboose

Is there a train-lover in your family or circle of friends? The odds are that your answer will be "yes", because locomotives seem to weave a web of attraction that enfolds model railroaders and aficionados of the real thing alike. And the caboose, celebrated in folk songs and children's tales, has a charm that appeals even to those of us who aren't among the locomotion faithful. We offer this bird house design as an emblem of enthusiasm for train buffs that may also enchant those of us who've never felt the call of the rhythm of the rails.

Virtually all of the pieces can be cut from 1x stock. The base (and its matching roof), for example, are 18" lengths of 1 x 8. The wheel blocks are among the few exceptions to this rule, each being a 4" section of 2 x 4. Use a hole saw to make the eight 1-1/2"-diameter wheels from scraps of 1x stock, and secure them to the blocks with no.8 x 1-1/2" brass flathead woodscrews.

Building upward, you'll need to cut two interior cab supports, each 1 x 1" x 4-1/2". These will fit inside the cab and provide a seat for the screws that hold it to the base. The sides of the cab are cut from 1 x 6, each measuring 14" long. Then, from the same 1 x 6 stock, you'll need to cut four 4-1/2" sections to serve as the ends and interior partitions.

The holes—centered 2" down from the top edge and spaced at 2-1/2", 7", and 11-1/2" intervals—are 1-1/2" in diameter. The outer two are "dummies", backed with scrap lumber and painted black to simulate openings. (We chose to block off the interior to create a single compartment of standard floor dimensions. Another alternative would be to make a three-apartment caboose for purple martins.) The partitions that create the dummy chambers are positioned 2-1/2" from each end of the cab. The perches are simply 2" pieces of 3/8" dowel, glued into 1/4"-deep 3/8" holes.

The upper cab is also cut from 1x stock. Its roof measures 7" x 7-1/2", its sides each 2-1/2" x 5-1/2", and its front and back panels each 2-1/4" x 4-1/2". (The latter are mounted flush to the roof of the main cab, leaving 1/4" vent slots along their top edges. Be sure, also, to drill four or five 3/8" vent holes in the roof beneath the upper cab, and a quartet of the same to drain the floor of the nesting compartment.)

The windows that trim both upper and lower cabs are cut from 1/4" plywood. The lower two each measure 2" x 3", those on the sides of the upper cab are each 1-1/4" x 2", and the single pane on the upper back measures 1" x 2".

The smokestack, a 2" piece of 5/8" dowel, is set into a drilled 1/4" x 1-1/2" x 3/4" base (cut from plywood). The roof trim is formed by ripping 3/4" dowel in half. The sections measure 8-3/4" and 4-1/4", each allowing a little overhang. Finally, the guard rails on the front and the rear of the base are formed from 3/16" steel rod, and pushed into pre-drilled holes.

Most of the assembly can be handled with glue and 8d galvanized finish nails (though you might prefer to paint the caboose before putting it together). The cab, however, is secured to its interior braces with easily removable no.8 x 1-1/2" brass flathead woodscrews.

We chose to paint our nest box in a sort of "generic caboose" red and black. If you'd like to get more adventurous, try to duplicate an actual caboose from a local line (or the one that brings up the rear of your personal train set).

Yes, the glory days of the rails might be behind us, but with air travel becoming less reliable and less affordable, perhaps our little red caboose will entice a few feathered frequent flyers to try something different . . . to take the train.

The Willow Wren

MATERIALS LIST

(2) 1 x 8 x 18" Pine
(2) 2 x 4 x 4" Pine
1 x 2" x 15" Pine
(2) 1 x 1" x 4-1/2" Pine
(2) 1 x 6 x 14" Pine
(4) 1 x 6 x 4-1/2" Pine
(3) 3/8" x 2" Dowels
1 x 7" x 7-1/2" Pine
(2) 1 x 2-1/2" x 5-1/2" Pine
(2) 1 x 2-1/4" x 4-1/2" Pine
(2) 1/4" x 2" x 3" Plywood
(2) 1/4" x 1-1/4" x 2" Plywood
1/4" x 1 x 2 Plywood
5/8" x 2" Dowel
1/4" x 1-1/2" x 3/4" Plywood
3/4" x 14" Dowel
3/16" x 16" Steel rod
8d Galvanized finish nails
(2) no.8 x 1-1/2" Brass flathead woodscrews

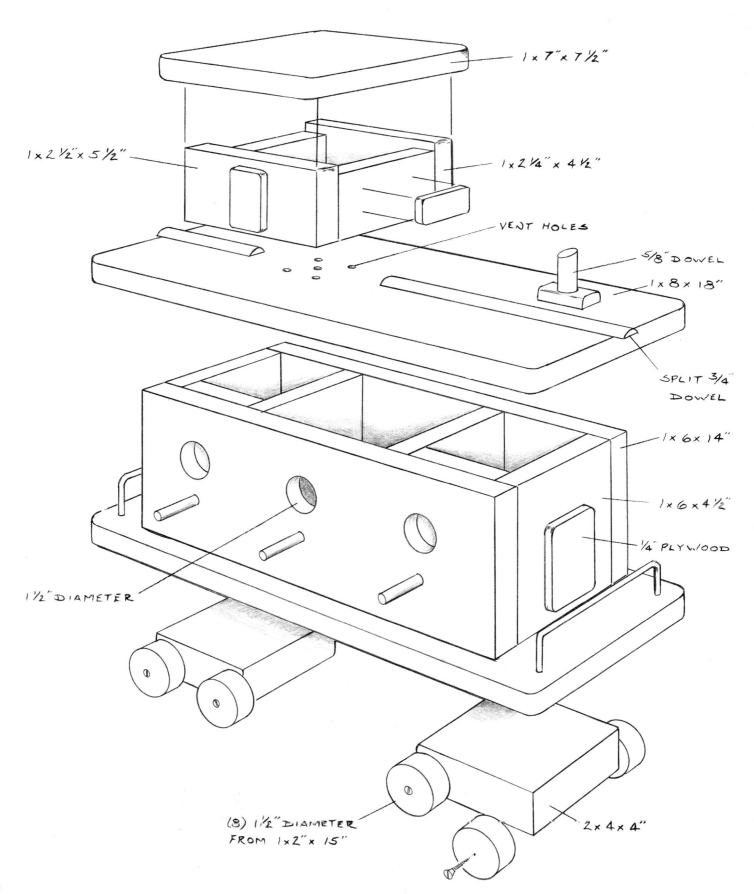

1 x 7" x 7½"

1 x 2½" x 5½"

1 x 2¼" x 4½"

VENT HOLES

5/8" DOWEL

1 x 8 x 18"

SPLIT ¾" DOWEL

1 x 6 x 14"

1 x 6 x 4½"

¼" PLYWOOD

1½" DIAMETER

(8) 1½" DIAMETER FROM 1 x 2" x 15"

2 x 4 x 4"

Ship of Fowls

Since Noah found land with the help of a dove, it seems appropriate that this miniature ark return the favor—by serving as a feeder or nesting platform for our feathered friends.

All of the components of this bird boat can be cut from 1x lumber. Begin by drawing one side on a 12 x 23" board. (Either use the template provided here, or sketch a suitably nautical shape freehand.) Use a jig saw, coping saw, or band saw to cut out one side, then use that board as a pattern to trace the shape for its duplicate.

The front and rear panels of the ark, again consisting of 1x stock, are each 6" x 9-1/2", with their tops and bottoms beveled 10° so they'll be horizontal when the planks are fastened in place. The deck measures 9-1/2" x 18" and has the same 10° bevel on each of its ends to allow the flush mounting of the front and rear panels. Also, to provide adequate drainage in foul weather, five saw kerfs—each centered, 12" long, and 1-1/2" apart—should be cut into the deck.

The cabin is also fairly simple to fashion. Its two sides are 7-1/2" x 9-3/4", each with a 45° bevel at one end to meet the roof. The front and back begin as 6" x 12-5/8" planks, which are then mitered to form the 90° peaks. Now, on each of these four panels, measure 5-1/2" up from the bottom and use that point to center a 4" hole saw. Bore the hole, and then run straight cuts from the holes' outer edges to complete the arches.

Finally, the roof consists of two 7" x 10" panels, each beveled 45° on its 10" sides. The ark can be painted either before or after assembling it with no. 8 x 1-1/2" brass flathead wood screws. Then, once you've decked the deck with a selection of plastic or wooden toy animals, you're ready to invite the birds to come...two by two.

MATERIALS LIST

1 x 12 x 23" Pine
(2) 1 x 6" x 9-1/2" Pine
1 x 9-1/2" x 18" Pine
(2) 1 x 7-1/2" x 9-3/4" Pine
(2) 1 x 6" x 12-5/8" Pine
(2) 1 x 7" x 10" Pine
(20) no.8 x 1-1/2" Brass flathead woodscrews

The Turtle Dove

Broad Boards

A few of the houses in this book use 1 x 12 lumber in their construction. These days it's not easy to find a quality board that wide, since old-growth forests are mostly gone, and second- and third-growth trees are harvested at a comparatively young age. If you can't locate kiln-dried, unwarped 1 x 12s, consider substituting plywood in this and other designs.

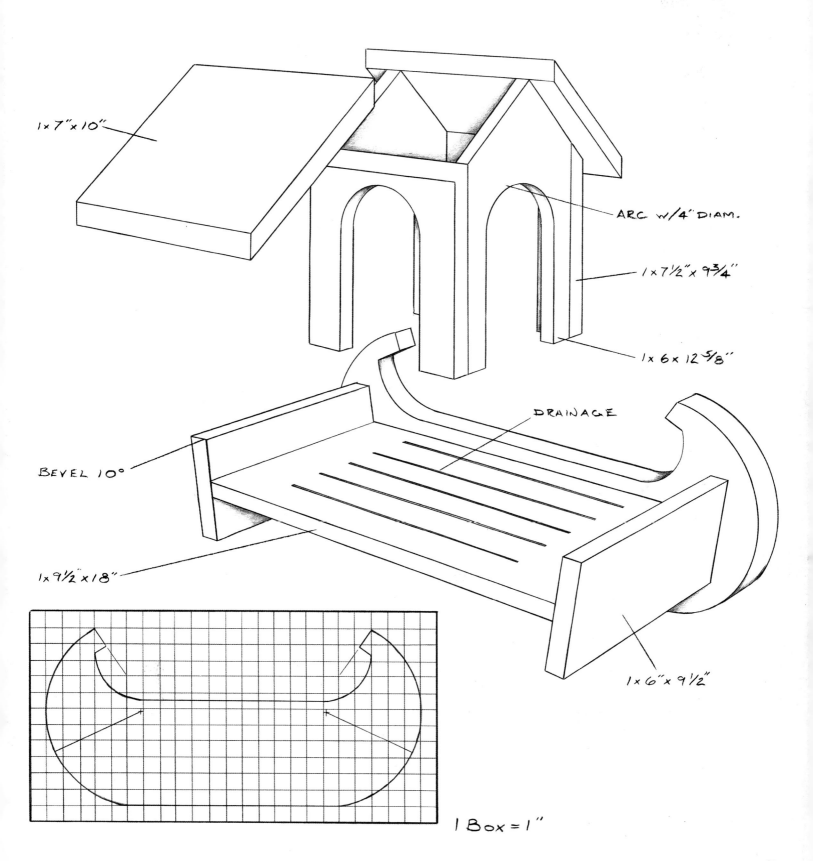

1x7"x10"

ARC W/4" DIAM.

1 x 7½" x 9¾"

1 x 6 x 12⁵⁄₈"

DRAINAGE

BEVEL 10°

1x9½"x18"

1 x 6"x 9½"

1 Box = 1"

The Skyrocket

You can celebrate with fireworks year around with this bird house, which perches atop its mounting pole as if waiting for an oversized match. And, though you'll get no star bursts from our rocket, we're betting that any bird with a sense of adventure will get a bang out of it!

MATERIALS LIST

(2) 1 x 8 x 26" Pine
(2) 1 x 6 x 22-1/2" Pine
(2) 1 x 8 x 8-1/2 Pine
1 x 4 x 32" Pine
1 x 2-3/4" x 5-1/4" Pine
(3) 1 x 3/4" x 2" Pine
1 x 5-3/8" x 5-5/8" Pine
(8) no.8 x 1-1/2" Brass
   flathead woodscrews
6d Galvanized finish nails
3/16" x 12" Steel rod

To begin, cut two 26" lengths of 1 x 8, and double miter one end of each to produce a 60° peak. Then designate one as the front of the rocket and, at a point 15" from the peak, cut it in two on a 45° bevel angling away from the peak. The two sides, cut from 1 x 6, measure 22-1/2" long. The roof can also be cut from 1 x 8 stock. Each side is 8-1/2" long, with a 30° bevel on its long edge.

You'll need a 32" length of 1 x 4 to make the fins. First draw a perpendicular line across the center, and then divide each of the two rectangles thus formed with another line, creating four right triangles. Measure 3" up from the 90° corner of each of these, and draw a line to angle across the 4" dimension to the larger acute corner. Finally, measure 3" down from the smaller acute angle of each, and draw a perpendicular line intersecting the hypotenuse. Now simply cut out the four fins thus drawn.

The Green Woodpecker

You'll need to turn to 1x scrap for the rest of the components. The awning that will cover the entry hole (which should be 1-1/2" in diameter and centered 7-1/2" below the peak) measures 2-3/4" x 5-1/4", with a 30° bevel on one long edge. It is supported by two 3/4" x 2" braces, each beveled to 30° at one end to meet the awning. The perch measures 3/4" x 2". And finally, the floor—which will be positioned 8-1/2" from the base of the rocket, and which should incorporate four evenly spaced 1/2" drainage holes—measures about 5-3/8" x 5-5/8". (This may be a loose fit, which is perfectly alright as it'll offer additional ventilation and drainage.)

Begin the assembly process by attaching the fins to the sides, from inside, with no.8 x 1-1/2" brass flathead wood screws. Then join the sides to the back with 6d galvanized finish nails. (Leave the gap at the top, as this will provide ventilation.) With that done, secure the floor on three sides, and then go on to fasten the upper front panel, the roof, the awning, and the perch in place with 6d galvanized finish nails.

Now slip the lower front panel into position, and drill three 3/16" holes, each 2-3/4" deep, through the panel and into the sides. Two of these should be on one side, the third on the other. Three 3-1/4" lengths of 3/16" steel rod, each with a 90 degree angle formed 3/4" from one end, can be pushed through these holes, securing the lower front while allowing easy access to the birdhouse's interior.

As you can see from our example, the rocket's paint scheme should provide a good opportunity to let your imagination run wild. We got our inspiration from roadside fireworks stands. You might take a similar approach, or simply coat the whole nest box in a "firecracker" red. Then again, you could choose more muted colors, in deference to the less adventurous birds that might thus be tempted to take up residence.

It's up to you. After all, the sky's the limit!

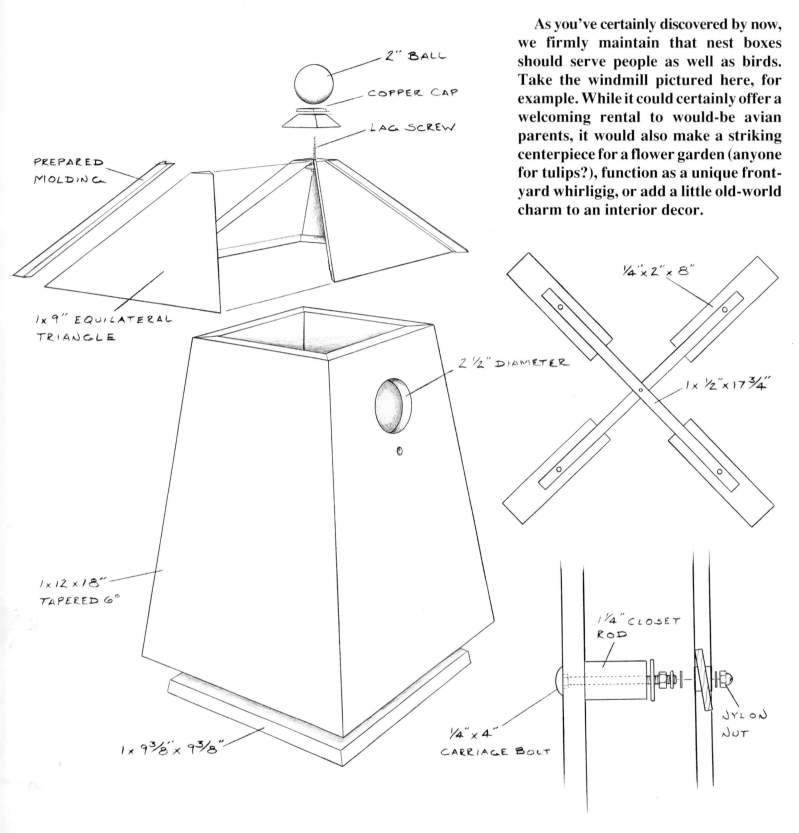

Dutch Treat

As you've certainly discovered by now, we firmly maintain that nest boxes should serve people as well as birds. Take the windmill pictured here, for example. While it could certainly offer a welcoming rental to would-be avian parents, it would also make a striking centerpiece for a flower garden (anyone for tulips?), function as a unique front-yard whirligig, or add a little old-world charm to an interior decor.

2" BALL

COPPER CAP

LAG SCREW

PREPARED MOLDING

1 x 9" EQUILATERAL TRIANGLE

2 ½" DIAMETER

¼" x 2" x 8"

1 x ½" x 17¾"

1 x 12 x 18" TAPERED 6°

1 x 9⅜" x 9⅜"

1¼" CLOSET ROD

¼" x 4" CARRIAGE BOLT

NYLON NUT

But you seldom get something for nothing, and the pleasingly simply lines of this birdhouse belie some fairly intricate construction steps.

The house itself isn't too imposing, however, and can all be cut from 1x lumber. Each side begins as a 1 x 12 x 18" board. The long edges are then ripped at a taper of about 6° to form a 7-1/2" x 11-1/4" x 18" trapezoid, with all long sides beveled to 45°. The mitered corners of the box can then be assembled with cabinet-maker's corner fasteners in the end grain at each open end. The base will measure 9-3/8" square, incorporate a 1/2" drainage hole near each corner, and have each side beveled to 6° to allow it to be slipped up into the larger end of the box. It should be secured with no.8 x 1-1/2" brass flathead wood screws, allowing its removal for cleaning. The hole (which we've put behind the blades for our photograph, but which you might want to place on the back of the house if you hope to attract birds) is centered 4-1/2" from the top, and is 2-1/2" in diameter.

The roof consists of four 9" equilateral triangles, each beveled to 45° on two of its adjoining sides. Come down 1-1/2" from each beveled peak, and cut off the point with your saw blade set at 45° to form a level platform for the peak ornament when the panels are assembled. To give the roof a seat on the base, dado a 1/4" deep, 5/8" step on the inside base of each roof panel. The roof probably won't require any further fastening, though you could glue it in place.

The roof ridges are capped with 1" x 1" x 7-7/8" trim, notched to conform to the ridges and beveled parallel at 45° at each end. It's easiest to start with a 32" length of 1" x 1" stock, cut the V-notch once, and then trim the strips to length. To cut the groove, set the blade angle to 45° and the height to 3/8", with the blade tip 1/2" from the rip fence. Run the stock through from one direction, flop it, and repeat to complete the notch.

The peak assembly consists of a 1/4" x 2-1/2" lag screw and fender washer; a 2-3/4" square 1x cap, beveled to 45° on all sides; a 2"-diameter wooden cabinet knob; and a 2" square of copper flashing. Once the roof is assembled with glue and/or 6d galvanized finish nails, the peak can be installed as shown in the illustration. (Be careful not to over tighten the knob on the lag screw, as the pressure on the washer will tend to pull apart the roof at its peak.)

The propeller axle assembly consists of a 1/4" x 4" carriage bolt, a 2" length of closet rod with a 5/16" hole drilled through its center (use a drill press if you have one), one 1/4" nylon nut, two 1/4" nylon washers, one 1/4" nylon cap nut . . . and, of course, the blades.

And what's a windmill without its sails? The blade arms measure 1 x 1/2" x 17-3/4", and are made by ripping 1/2" off a length of 1x stock. To cut the notches to accept the blades, simply set your saw blade to 10° and make 5-1/4" cuts, centered on the 1/2" dimension, into the ends of the crosspieces. Now cut 3/4" dados, 1/4" deep, centered on each arm (keep the angle on the airfoils in mind when planning these cuts), and glue the arms together before drilling a 1/4" axle hole at their center. The blades are simply 1/4" x 2" x 8" strips of lattice, fastened with glue and, if you feel the need for more security, one or two 3/16" copper rivets apiece.

Your plans for the windmill will likely influence its paint scheme. If it's to decorate a yard, flower bed, or living room, make it as bright and as intricate as your patience and abilities allow. If you hope to attract residents, however, you'd be better served by muted tones and might even want to leave it to weather naturally. Should you take the latter approach, however, do position the entry hole in the back of the house, or lock the blades in a stationary position, lest your would-be tenants risk becoming grist for your mill!

MATERIALS LIST

(4) 1 x 12 x 18" Pine
1 x 9-3/8" x 9-3/8" Pine
(4) no.8 x 1-1/2 Brass
    flathead woodscrews
(4) 1 x 9" x 9" Pine
(4) 1" x 1" x 7-7/8" Pine
1/4" x 2-1/2" Lag screw
1/4" Fender washer
1 x 2-3/4" x 2-3/4" Pine
2" Cabinet knob
2" x 2" Copper flashing
6d Galvanized finish nails
1/4" x 4" Carriage bolt
2" Closet rod
(2) 1/4" Nylon wawshers
1/4" Nylon nut
1/4" Nylon cap nut
(2) 1 x 1/2" x 17-3/4" Pine
(4) 1/4" x 2" x 8" Lattice
(8) 3/16" Copper rivets

A Tudor Coop

To our way of thinking, there are few more homey looking house designs than the classic Tudor cottage. This nest box is an attempt to translate that warm charm in miniature—to create a bird house that's as appealing as it is practical, and that's subtle enough in color and trim to attract the most timid of species.

The Black-Headed Bunting

Thatch

If you'd like to take this house one step further, adding real thatch is the logical choice. Consider weaving together sprigs of dried grasses, or, for a ready solution, sacrifice a whisk broom to your Tudor's roof.

69

MATERIALS LIST

3/4" x 8-1/4" x 8-1/4" OSB
3/4" x 7-3/4" x 8-1/4" OSB
3/4" x 2-1/2" x 8-1/4" OSB
3/4" x 1-3/4" x 8-1/4" OSB
1/2" x 6" x 11" Plywood
(2) 1/2" x 6" x 6-1/2"
    Plywood
1/2" x 4" x 6" Plywood
1 x 5" x 2" Pine
1/2" x 5" x 7-1/2" Plywood
(2) 3/4" Outside corner
    molding, 4" long
(2) 3/4" Outside corner
    molding, 2-3/4" long
(2) 3/4" Outside corner
    molding, 6-3/4" long
1 x 1/4" x 48" Pine
1/4" x 3" x 3" Plywood
3/4" x 5" x 5" Plywood
(4) no.8 x 1-1/4" Brass
flathead woodscrews
6d Galvanized finish nails

The cottage's roof is built from 3/4" oriented strand board (commonly called OSB), which provides an easy and effective means of suggesting the Tudor thatched roof. One side measures 8-1/4" x 8-1/4", and has a 60° bevel on one edge. The other is a 7-3/4" x 8-1/4" rectangle, with the 60° bevel on one long side. When they're assembled, the bevel of the shorter piece is simply butted against the face of the longer, with the bevel on the larger panel extending the slope of the former and completing the peak.

The roof cap is formed in the same manner, and consists of one 2-1/2" x 8-1/4" strip of OSB and a second strip measuring 1-3/4" x 8-1/4". All of the exposed edges of the roof pieces should be rounded on a sander to give the appearance of thatch.

The back wall (and all the other structural walls) is cut from 1/2" plywood. It begins as a 6" x 11" panel, with a double miter cut at the top to create the 60° peak. Each side wall measures 6" x 6-1/2", with a 30° bevel cut at the top. To produce the cantilever (for the overhanging "second floor"), simply cut a 1-1/2" x 4-3/4" notch from one of the 6" sides of each panel.

The "first floor" front wall measures 4" x 6", and is topped with a 1 x 5" x 2" sill, positioned across the top and extending forward enough to allow the gable wall to be secured to it while sliding between the side walls. The latter piece, again cut from 1/2" plywood, is 5" x 7-1/2", with a 60° peak mitered on one short end. (Give extra care to these cuts, as the slope of the gable wall must meet that of the bevel on the side walls, with only 3/4" corner molding to cover errors.)

All of the house's corners are trimmed with 3/4" outside corner molding. The lower front wall needs two 4" sections; the upper front will require two 2-3/4" lengths, each mitered to 30° at one end to meet the slope of the roof; and the rear will take two 6-3/4" strips with 30° miters at their upper ends.

The rest of the cottage's trim is formed by ripping 1/4" strips from 1x stock, then cutting these to fit. Use the illustration as a key; all of the angles will be either 45°, 60° or 90°.

The hole, positioned 5-1/2" on center from the peak of the second-story front, measures 1-1/2" in diameter. It receives its own piece of trim, cut from 1/4" plywood. To make this piece, first cut a disk with a 2-1/2" hole saw, then switch to a 1-1/2" hole saw, using the same pilot hole.

The base of the bird house should be cut from 3/4" plywood, and measures 5" x 5", with a quartet of 1/2" drainage holes, one near each corner. It'll be installed last, and can be secured in place with no.8 x 1-1/4" brass flathead wood screws, allowing its removal for cleaning.

Considering the complexity of the trim, you'll probably want to first check the fit of all pieces, then paint or stain them dark before final assembly. Leave the roof natural, and choose earthy colors with good contrast for the walls and trim. Be sure, as always, to use good exterior-grade paints if the house will actually be used to attract birds.

Once the pieces have dried, assemble them with glue, using 6d galvanized finish nails where required for strength.

After you've built your first Tudor bird house, you may be tempted to assemble more, perhaps even to market a few at a local crafts outlet. If so, more power to you; there's many a big business that started out as a "cottage" industry!

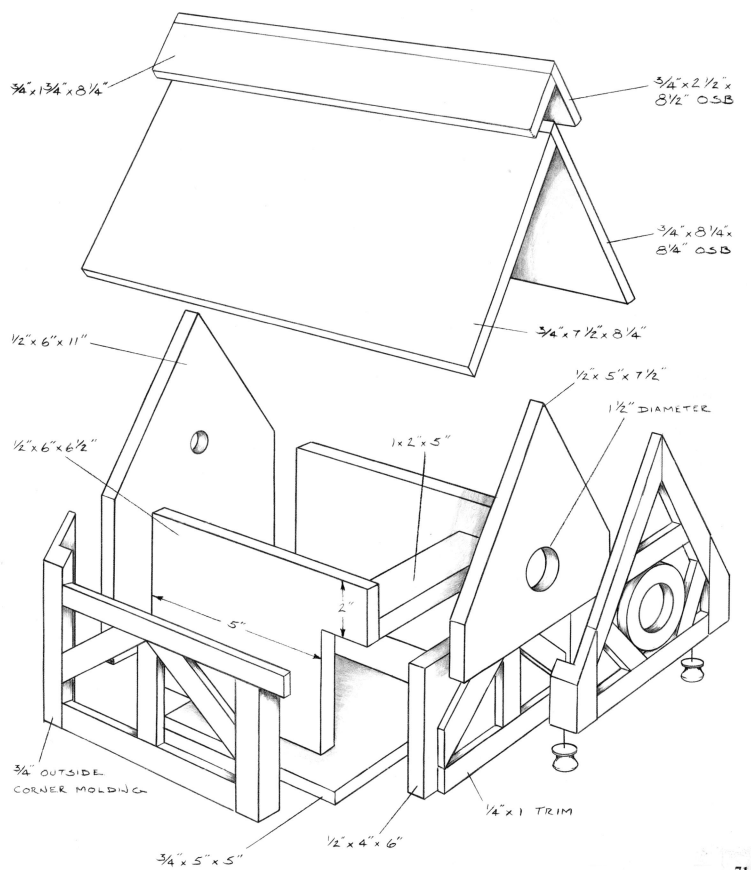

3/4" x 1 3/4" x 8 1/4"

3/4" x 2 1/2" x 8 1/2" OSB

3/4" x 8 1/4" x 8 1/4" OSB

1/2" x 6" x 11"

3/4" x 7 1/2" x 8 1/4"

1/2" x 5" x 7 1/2"

1 1/2" DIAMETER

1/2" x 6" x 6 1/2"

1 x 2" x 5"

2"

5"

3/4" OUTSIDE CORNER MOLDING

1/4" x 1 TRIM

3/4" x 5" x 5"

1/2" x 4" x 6"

The Cuckoo Condo

Talk about life imitating art imitating life. The original Black Forest cuckoo clock could easily be said to mimic bird houses, with the nesting cuckoo emerging from its chamber to sing the changes of the hours, while our nest box places a family of wrens in a wooden cuckoo's role, if only to mark the changing of the seasons.

The basic bird house, to which the decorative front face and trim will be attached, is cut from 1/2" plywood. Each half of the roof consists of a 7" x 8" rectangle, with one of its long sides mitered at 45° to form half of the right-angled peak. Each side panel is a simple 6" x 6-1/2" block. (These are not mitered and will be mounted flush with the base in order to leave ventilation slots under the roof.) The front and back walls begin as 5" x 10-1/2" rectangles, then are mitered to form a 90° point.

The false front begins as a 9-1/4" x 15-3/4" piece of 3/4" ply. Use your miter gauge to cut a 90° peak on one end, then draw a line across the base of that triangle, find its center, and mark points 3" from each side of it. Line up those points with their respective lower corners, and scribe two lines, each stretching the full length of the board, to mark the sloping sides. Then cut along these lines.

Now mark the center point of the base and, positioning a 4"-diameter can lid in such a way that it's centered and just touching the mark, trace the hemisphere that will form the bottom of the decorative scroll. Place the same jar lid on one side of the hemisphere, so that 1/4 of its arc swings from the upper edge of the half circle to the side of the panel, and trace that arc. Do the same on the far side. Use a jig saw, coping saw, or band saw to cut along the lines, being careful to cut into the two sharp angles (where the curves meet) from one side before backing out the blade and completing the cut from the other direction. (You'll probably need to clean up these cuts later with a file or sandpaper.)

The two trim pieces that hang beneath the roof are cut from 3" x 6-1/2" pieces of 1/2" plywood. Miter one end of each to 45°, then trace your pattern on one, cut it out, and use the finished piece as a template for the other side. The peak cap is made from two 8"-long pieces of joint (or seam) molding ripped at 45°. Set the rip fence so that the blade will just remove one of the two smaller bumps.

Assemble the components as shown, using glue and 6d galvanized finish nails. (You might want to use no.8 x 1-1/4" brass flathead wood screws to secure the base so it can be removed for cleaning.) Go on to drill one 1/2" drainage hole near each corner of the base, and bore the 1-1/2" entry hole through both the false front and the front wall.

Now paint the clock to your liking. It could be colored a rich, chocolate brown with bright Tyrolean floral scroll work for decoration, or you could do as we did and simply treat all of the pieces with a rich, dark stain for a more natural, and traditional, look. Finally, cut a short section of stout spring, bore a small hole to accept a straightened length of one end of it, and glue the spring in place. The perch is simply a paddle of 1/2" plywood, shaped in such a way that its smaller end can be "screwed" into the coil. Stain or paint it to match the rest of the bird house.

The clock's face can be painted on as ours is. However, should you feel unequal to attempting the numerals, simply salvage an old alarm clock from a secondhand shop and cannibalize it's face and hands.

And, in no time at all, you're done. Hang it up. We think you'll soon discover that a wren in your own backyard beats a cuckoo in the Black Forest . . . (ahem) hands down.

The Cuckoo

MATERIALS LIST

(2) 1/2" x 7" x 8" Plywood
(2) 1/2" x 6" x 6-1/2" Plywood
(2) 1/2" x 5" x 10-1/2" Plywood
3/4" x 9-1/4" x 15-3/4" Plywood
(2) 1/2" x 3" x 6-1/2" Plywood
(4) no.8 x 1-1/4" Brass flathead woodscrews
Steel coil spring
1/2" Plywood scrap

A-Frame Chalet

So ornate, you can almost smell the gingerbread . . . . If you enjoy detail work, you'll have a field day with this chalet. What our builder has done here is essentially to turn blocks of wood into sculpture using powertools.

The frame of the house is simple enough to construct. Two 8" x 16" sections of 3/8" plywood make up the roof, and a triangle of 3/4" plywood set in a 1/16"-deep dado groove supports them.

Cutting the bevel in the roof panels at the peak does require a special technique on most tablesaws. To achieve the 19° bevel, the panels must be run through the tablesaw vertically, sliding against the rip fence. However, the point emerging from the back of the blade will be prone to drop into the blade slot, causing a dangerous jam. To avoid this, slide the plywood through on top of a sacrificial board. (You'll have to put a spacer between the plywood and the fence.)

Once you've beveled the peak, run the other ends through the saw with the boards lying flat (long side up) and the blade set at the same angle. Now adjust your dado for 3/4" width and 1/16" depth, and groove the inside of each roof panel 1/2" from the back.

The back of the roof assembly is a 38° isosceles triangle with an 8-1/4" base. Cut this board from 3/4" plywood, and glue it into the dados in the 3/8" roof panels, gluing the peak at the same time.

Now prepare two 1/2"-plywood triangles of the same dimensions as the 3/4" back. In one of them, drill the 1-1/2" entry hole 8" below the peak. To increase the depth of the entry hole, use hole saws to make a 1-1/2" x 2-1/4" ring from 3/8" plywood, and glue it over the entry hole. The two 1/2" triangles overlap a 1/2" x 4" x 8-1/4" plywood base, which has 19° bevels on each of its 4" sides. Assemble these boards, adding a 4" scrap of 1x stock near the peak for support. This main unit slides up into the roof and is held in place by a screw through each roof panel and into the base.

All the trim is permanently attached to the 1/2"-plywood main unit. Starting from the top, cut out a 38° triangle with a 2-1/4" base from 1x stock. Bevel the 2-1/4" side 45° so it won't show. The detail elements are all rendered on a 3/8" plywood triangle with a base of 4". The two arcs at the bottom are made with a 1-1/2" hole saw, and the three blue dots are just shallow holes made with a 3/8" rotary rasp. The 3/4" descending ball (from a craft store) is attached to the plywood triangle with 3/16" dowel.

Believe it or not, with the exception of the 1/2" balls, the entire porch railing started as a piece of 2 x 2-1/2" stock. A combination of tablesaw cuts and dados, along with holes and arcs bored with 5/8" and 1-1/8" bits, rendered this remarkable transformation. The profile drawing should help you work out a facsimile of the piece you see in the photo.

The lower trim piece is 3/8" plywood, 1-3/4" high bored with a 2" bit. The two balls are 3/4", and the button screw hole plugs cover two no.6 x 1" woodscrews that anchor the trim to the main unit.

Slide the finished main unit up into the roof, and countersink a no. 6 hole through each roof panel and into 1/2" plywood base of the main unit. A pair of no.6 x 1" screws hold the assembly solidly together, while leaving it easy to open for cleaning.

No other house in this collection offers such an open invitation to fancy when it comes to painting. Our painter definitely got into the spirit of it, and we imagine you will too.

MATERIALS LIST

(2) 3/8" x 8" x 16" Plywood
3/4" x 8-1/4" x 12" Plywood
(2) 3/8" x 8-1/4" x 12" Plywood
3/8" x 2" x 2" Plywood
3/8" x 4" x 8-1/4" Plywood
1 x 2-1/4" x 3" Pine
3/8" x 4" x 5-1/2" Plywood
2 x 2-1/2" x 7" Pine
3/8" x 1-3/4" x 9" Plywood
(3) 3/4" Wooden balls
(3) 1/2" Wooden balls
(2) Button screw hole plugs
(4) no. 6 x 1" Brass flathead woodscrews

The Barred Woodpecker

Pancho's Villa

When we were building the bird houses that make up this book, friends frequently dropped by the shop to check on our progress. Almost without exception, their attention quickly focused upon this little hacienda. And that was both surprising and gratifying, because our adobe abode is among the simplest designs we've attempted.

To begin, cut two 2'-lengths of 2 x 8, and edge-glue and clamp them to form the base. When the assembly is dry, cut off one section 9-1/2" long for the roof, leaving 14-3/8" for the base. Next, rip the 9-1/2" section of doubled 2 x 8 down to a width of 11". The front and back walls are simply 8"-long pieces cut from 2 x 8 lumber, with the entry hole—sized and positioned to suit a particular bird species—drilled

The Sand Martin

77

LIST OF MATERIALS

- (2) 2 x 8 x 9-1/2" Pine
- (2) 2 x 8 x 14-3/8" Pine
- (2) 2 x 8 x 11" Pine
- (2) 2 x 8 x 8" Pine
- (5) 1-1/4"-long 5/8" Dowels
- (2) 8-1/4"-long 3/4" Dowels
- (1) 1 x 2" x 8" Mahogany
- (2) 1 x 1" x 3-1/4" Mahogany
- (2) No. 12 x 2-1/2" Brass flathead woodscrews
- 8d Galvanized finish nails
- Brick-facade adhesive

in one of them with the appropriate hole saw.

We decided to shape the side walls and roof on a tablesaw to give the house the free-form feel of adobe. You might want to eliminate this step, or simply round the corners and roof edges with a rasp or belt sander. Either way, cut an 11"-length of 2 x 8 for each wall. Then, if you choose to go our route, you'll want to taper each wall to 1" on a tablesaw. You'll have to cut the taper in from each side, then break off the trimmed section and sand any roughness from the broken joint, since the saw cuts won't quite meet in the center. Then, taper the 11"-long sides of the roof board, again using the table saw, to match the slope of the side walls.

With that done, select a 5/8" drill bit and bore five holes about 1/2" deep on the front edge of the roof to accommodate the dowel "vigas" that protrude from the eave, and two more 3/4" in diameter in the base—each centered 4" from the front edge, and 5" from a side—to accept the dowel pillars.

Now assemble the front and side walls and the roof of the structure with glue and nails, recessing the front wall about 2" underneath the eaves. Then insert scraps of dowel into the

holes to prevent their getting plugged up while using a wide putty knife to "texture" the surface of the villa with brick-facade adhesive. Leave the back wall off, but coat one side of it with adhesive, too. It'll later be slipped into the space and secured with two No. 12 x 2-1/2" brass flathead woodscrews from below to allow its removal for cleaning.

There are a number of ways to go from here. You might, for example, simply let the adhesive dry as it is, or dust the house while it's wet with fine sand, or wait until it's thoroughly dried and paint the villa with a suitable earth-toned exterior paint. The base should be treated with the same material and painted tan or an earthy red to suggest the sun-baked Southwestern desert soil.

Then stain five 5/8"-diameter x 1-1/4"-long dowels and glue them into the holes in the roof. The pillars consist of 3/4"-diameter x 8-1/4"-long dowels. Each fits into an assembly built up from 1x stock. We happened to have some mahogany scraps in the shop, which we cut down to 2" wide x 8" long for the lintel, and to 1" wide x 3-1/4" long, each end cut at a 45° angle, for the twin corbels. These have 3/4" holes about 1/2" deep to accept the pillars. Finally, it's time to landscape the yard with a plastic cactus (you'll probably be able to find one in a toy department or hobby shop.)

And that's that. It's easy to add a touch of the great Southwest to your backyard. It'll provide a *fiesta* for your eyes, and a *siesta* for weary warblers.

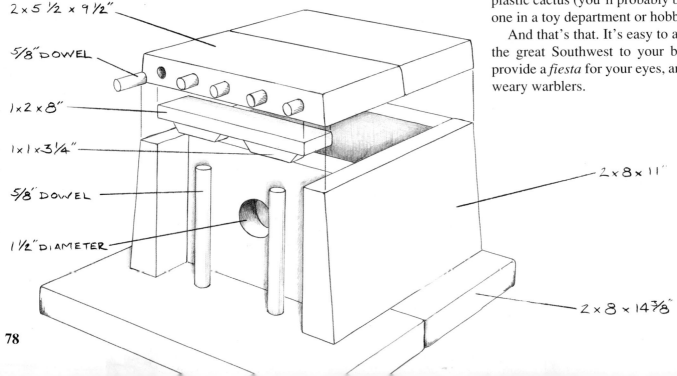

2 x 5 1/2 x 9 1/2"
5/8" DOWEL
1 x 2 x 8"
1 x 1 x 3 1/4"
5/8" DOWEL
1 1/2" DIAMETER
2 x 8 x 11"
2 x 8 x 14 3/8"

The Cupola

While our purple-martin penthouse is unquestionably the most ambitious project in this book, it also vies for top awards in drama and practicality. Worthy in its own regard as architectural ornamentation, it offers martins a cozy but well-ventilated nesting shelter far from terrestrial hazards. And, lest you be intimidated, consider that for the most part the techniques used to build the cupola are no more involved than those used on other houses in this book. It's just bigger!

Construction of the cupola can conveniently be divided into the roof assembly and the body of the house itself. So, starting from the bottom, let's rev up the tablesaw.

Base: The base of the cupola is a 21"-square box made of 3/4" plywood sides that are mitered together. Two sides are rectangular, while the other two have Vs cut to match the pitch of the roof the bird house is to be mounted on. Our example is for a 12-in-12 (or 45°) roof, but you'll need to adjust to suit your own case.

Bore the 2-1/2" entry holes before assembling the house. The rectangular sides get one hole up (centered left-right and 6-1/2" below the upper edge) and three down (centered 3-3/4", 10-1/2" and 17-1/4" from a side and 13-1/4" below the upper edge). This pattern reverses on the notched sides, with the trio of holes above. Once the holes are drilled, use glue and cabinetmaker's (or chevron) plywood corner fasteners to assemble the box. To provide for mounting, cut two 19-1/2" lengths of 2 x 4 and nail them into the V so that the broad face is flush with the edge. Drill a pair of 3/8" holes 18" apart in each board to accept lag screws.

Since this is a two-story residence, you'll need two 19-1/2"-square 3/4" plywood floors. Bore a 4" hole in the center of each floor to form the central ventilation shaft. To form the 6"-square apartments, cut out eight sections of 3/4" plywood 7-1/2" high and 19-1/2" long.

These will be lapped, as in egg-crate construction, by centering 3-3/4"-deep, 3/4"-wide mortises 6-3/8" from each end. The joints should fit tightly enough that no glue or fasteners are necessary. Before assembling the partitions, drill three or four 1/2" holes toward the top of the center 6" section of each board, so each compartment can ventilate into the central shaft.

The floors should rest, unfastened, on a ledge made of 3/4" x 3/4" stock, so they can be removed for installation and later for cleaning. Position the upper surface of the bottom floor 15-3/4" above the top of the base. The second story will rest on the first-floor partitions.

The trim on the lower section is much less complicated than it first looks. There are two mitered bands of joint molding (sometimes called seam molding) located 8-7/8" and 15-3/4" from the top. And wrapping around the top is a mitered band of 1 x 4 stock with a bevel on its lower edge, and two 1/8"-deep saw kerfs 1/2" and 1" up from the bevel.

Roof: Use 3/4" plywood to form the 28"-square base of the roof pyramid. When you cut this piece, set the saw blade to 22° to match the roof slope. Drill five or six 1" holes in the center of this board to allow the ventilation shaft to connect with the roof.

Each roof panel is a 3/8"-plywood 68° isosceles triangle that measures 28" on the base and has a 35" height. The tip is cut off parallel to the base at a point 32-1/2" up, to leave a 2" side. (Since the joints between these panels are covered by trim, we didn't bother to bevel the edges. Should you decide to do so, be sure to add 3/4" to the width.)

The four panels come together at the top on a square of 2x stock that's tapered to 68° (to match the roof slope) and measures 2" x 2" on its smaller end. Atop that assembly goes a square of 2 x 6 x 5-1/2", beveled 1/2" at 45° top and bottom, with an inch nipped off each point and decorative 1/8"-deep saw kerfs on its vertical faces. Nail the larger piece onto the pyramid, and drill a 1-1/4" hole through the center of it and the tapered 2" x 2" square.

MATERIALS LIST

- (4) 3/4" x 21" x 30" Plywood
- (2) 2 x 4 x 19-1/2" Pine
- (8) 1 x 3/4" x 19-1/2" Pine
- (2) 3/4" x 19-1/2" x 19-1/2" Plywood
- (8) 3/4" x 7-1/2" x 19-1/2" Plywood
- (8) 22-9/16"-long Joint molding
- (4) 1 x 4 x 22-91/6" Pine
- 3/4" x 28" x 28" Plywood
- (4) 28"-base, 68°, 3/8" Plywood isosceles triangles
- 2 x 3-7/32" x 3-7/32" Pine
- 2 x 6 x 5-1/2" Pine
- (4) 2 x 3-3/4" x 3-3/4" Pine
- (4) 2" Eave vent screens
- 2x Scrap Pine
- 12" x 12" 20 ga. Copper sheet
- (4) 2 x 2" x 34" Pine
- (2) 2 x 2 x 28" Pine
- (8) 1-1/6" x 28" Quarter round
- Drip edge
- Roll roofing
- Cabinetmaker's (or chevron) corner fasteners
- 6d Galvanized finish nails
- 8d Galvanized finish nails
- Copper brads
- (4) 3/8" x 3" Lag screws

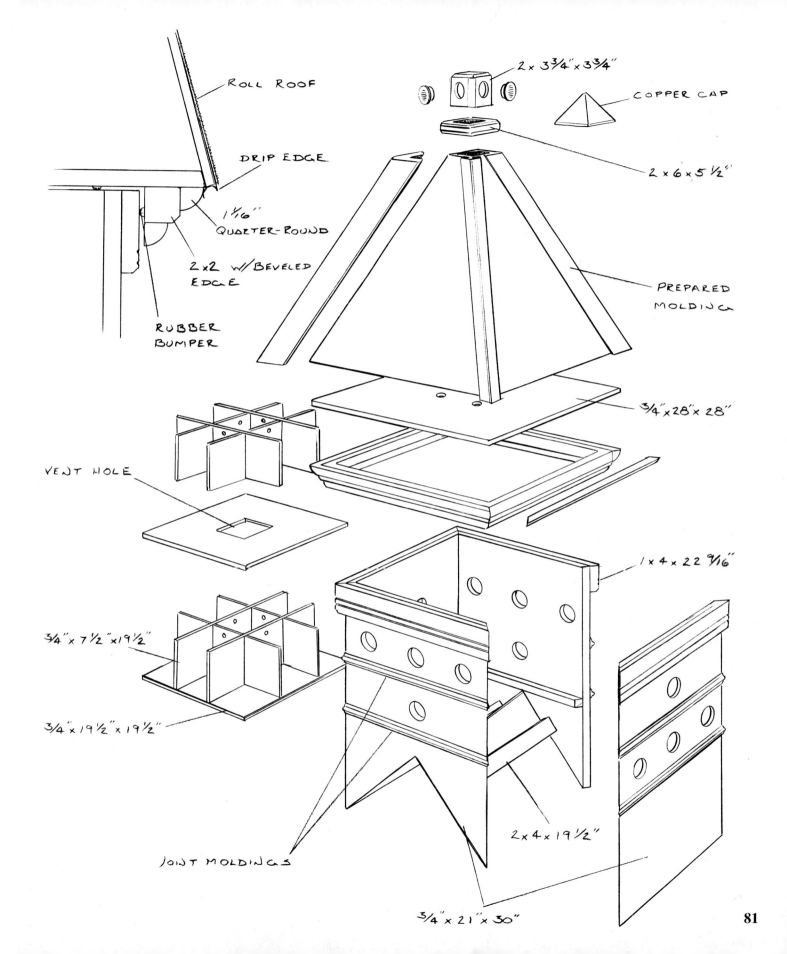

ROLL ROOF

DRIP EDGE

1¼₁₆″
QUARTER-ROUND

2 x 2 W/BEVELED
EDGE

RUBBER
BUMPER

2 x 3¾″ x 3¾″

COPPER CAP

2 x 6 x 5½″

PREPARED
MOLDING

3/4″ x 28″ x 28″

VENT HOLE

3/4″ x 7½″ x 19½″

3/4″ x 19½″ x 19½″

1 x 4 x 22 9/16″

JOINT MOLDINGS

2 x 4 x 19½″

3/4″ x 21″ x 30″

81

More mitered 2x makes up the cupola's cupola. You'll need to cut four pieces 3-3/4" square. Then saw dual 45° bevels on two parallel sides and a full 45° on the top of each one. In the center of each piece, bore a 2" hole, and press in an eave vent (available from any lumberyard). Now nail the parts together and use the assembly as a template to mark the location of its inside on the 2x below. Nail and glue small triangles of scrap to serve as nailers at the inside corners of this square, and complete the installation. Top the whole thing with a copper sheet-metal pyramid tacked in place with copper nails.

Roof trim consists of about 12' of 2 x 2" stock with multiple bevels. Start by setting the tablesaw blade to a 15° tilt, and then position the rip fence 1-11/16" from the base of the blade. Lay the 2 X 2" on the table with a 2" face down and run it through. Flip the board around and repeat the process. Now change the blade tilt to 45°, set the height to 3/8", and position the rip fence 1/2" from the base of the blade.

Run the 2 x 2" through with the remaining 2" face down, flipping it around to complete a V in the underside. Miter the ends of the four approximately 34" pieces at 22°, cutting and testing the fit until they're the right size. Nail them to the 3/8" plywood roof deck.

Trim under the eaves is, once again, deceptively simple. Just take 2 x 2 and cut a 1/2", 45° bevel on the lower, outside edge. Complement this with sections of 1-1/16" quarter round above and beneath the 2 x 2 stock.

We chose roll roofing for our cupola, but you'll probably want to use the same material that's on your home's roof. In any event, install "drip edge" strips along the lower edge of the roof, and be sure the roofing material (whatever it may be) laps all the way underneath the roof trim.

The roof assembly is substantial enough that it's unlikely to blow off in anything less than a hurricane. If you're concerned, though, you could include eyes and hooks to connect the base and roof section. Do be sure to leave at least 1/8" ventilation space between the two assemblies, though. We used rubber bumpers to stand the roof away from the base, but many other approaches would serve as well.

Mounting the cupola is not near as difficult as safely negotiating its considerable bulk up onto the roof. Get help for the hauling, or hire someone who's comfortable working on a steep roof. Mounting is simply a matter of sinking four 3/8" x 3" lag screws into the holes in the 2 x 4 mounting boards, through the roof, and into rafters below.

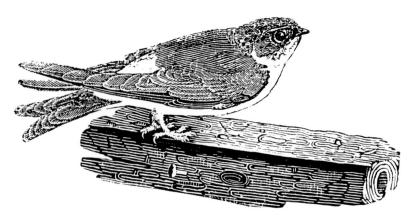

The Martin

Colonial Townhouse

Perfectly suited to sparrows, the 10" x 10" interior floor plan of this classic townhouse also makes excellent use of standard material sizes. Let your whimsy dictate the yard plan—perhaps you lean more toward rockers than chaize lounges—but do be sure to use waterproof glue where the base intersects the walls, and do include drain holes in the platform near the walls.

At first glance, the detail in this bird house may seem daunting. In reality, though, the house's admittedly numerous small pieces can rapidly be mass produced by preparing stock of the right configuration and trimming off slices, as if it was a loaf of bread.

The picket fence, for example, is a piece of 1 x 3 (actual dimensions of 25/32" x 2-1/2") ripped twice on a tablesaw with the blade set at 45° to form the point. Then 3/16"-thick slices are removed from the stock on a tablesaw or with a mitre box. All 42 pickets can be produced in 15 minutes.

Likewise, the siding can be ripped from 2x (actual thickness of 1-1/2") material to allow 1" of each piece of siding to reveal. Fifteen pieces, each about 4' long, will be enough to cover all the walls of the house. They are cut carefully to fit, then glued into place from bottom to top.

Nearly all the other detail pieces in the house are formed from 1/4" stock. If you have a thickness planer, you can make your own from 1x material. A simpler solution, though, is to buy 1/4" x 1- 1/2" lattice at the lumberyard. Rip about 4 feet of this molding down to 3/4" width for the fascia on the gable ends, and then slice off about 16 feet of 1/8"-thick pieces to form the 1/8" x 1/4" stock for the rails in the picket fence and the sash dividers in the windows. Make up about 16 feet of 3/8" x 1/4" stock for the window and door casings.

Perhaps the most intimidating part of building this bird house is working at such close quarters with the tablesaw blade. This is a time to pay particular attention to the section on safety (page 30). A push stick is mandatory, and feather sticks beside and above the stock will ensure accurate results.

The lap joints in the pickets and window frames are not entirely necessary, but they make assembly much easier and add strength. You'll probably want to make these cuts with the small pieces of wood set in a larger piece of stock. Just dado a groove of the appropriate depth and width in a piece of 1 x 6 and set the tiny pieces into the groove for a run through the saw blade.

Copper makes a lovely roof, and it is quite durable, but birds would probably be just as happy with galvanized steel, which is less expensive and readily available. Your best bet for finding copper is a custom sheet-metal shop; galvanized will also be available there or at a heating and air-conditioning supply. The metal on this house is backed up by a layer of fiberboard for support. This wouldn't be necessary if the roof was permanently affixed. In this design, however, the roof was the most logical place for cleanout access. The roof attaches to the house by two studs threaded into the crossbar and passing through the roof and each chimney.

Because of the siding, the hole gets an extension donut on the outside as well as the inside. The inner one is from 3/4" plywood, while the outer is from the 3/8" wall material.

Wondering about the door? It's just a piece of tempered hardboard with a 3/4" hole filled with leftover sash parts, glued to the front wall.

MATERIALS LIST

4' x 4' x 3/8" Plywood
2' x 2' x 3/4" Plywood
1 x 3 x 2' Fir
2 x 6 x 4' Fir
(2) 1/4" x 1-1/2" x 8' Lattice
(1) 1/4" x 1-1/16" Outside corner molding
2' x 2' Tempered hardboard
12" x 18" Copper (approx. 20 gauge)
(2) 1/4"-20 x 1-1/2" Brass bolts and nuts
(2) No. 8 x 1-1/4" Roundhead woodscrews
4d Galvanized finish nails

Colors?

Perhaps this one ought to go along with your own home's scheme. After all, with a little imagination you could visualize the hole as a porthole window and see children playing on the stair landing between the first and second stories.

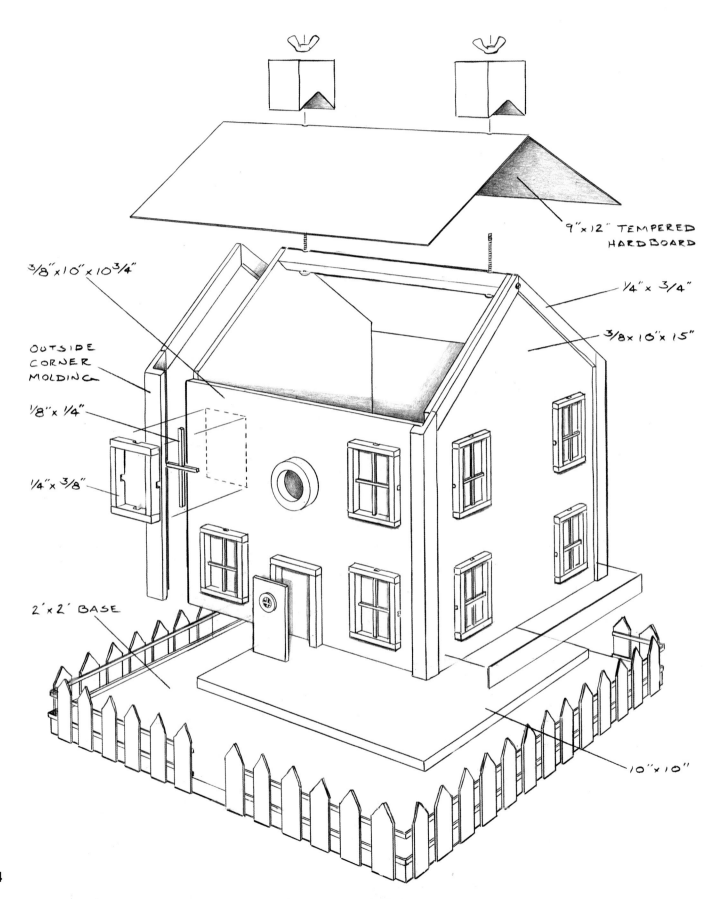

9"x12" TEMPERED HARDBOARD

3/8"x10"x10³/4"

1/4" x 3/4"

3/8 x10"x 15"

OUTSIDE
CORNER
MOLDING

1/8"x 1/4"

1/4"x 3/8"

2'x2' BASE

10"x10"

84

The One-Room Schoolhouse

MATERIALS LIST

1/2" x 10" x 10-1/2"
  Plywood
1/2" x 11" x 12-1/4"
  Plywood
3/4" x 10" x 10" Plywood
1/2" x 11" x 16-1/2"
  Plywood
(4) 1/4" x 3/4" x 11" Outside
  corner molding
(4) 1/4" x 3/4" x 7-3/4" Pine
1/4" x 5" x 5" Pine
2 x 2-1/4" x 7" Pine
(2) 3/8" x 1/2" x 2-1/2" Fir
(2) 3/8" x 1/2" x 4-1/2" Fir
(8) Doll house porch posts
1/4" x 2-1/2" x 5" Plywood
2 x 2-1/4" x 4-1/2" Pine
(2) 1/4" x 1-3/4" x 3"
  Plywood
3/8" x 3/8" x 2" Fir
3/8" x 3/8" x 5/8" Fir
1/2" x 1/2" x 4-1/8" Fir
1/2" x 1/2" x 1-1/2" Fir

The Little Owl

You've heard the expression "wise as an owl." This is one school where you learn by being outside and looking in. You can put a pair (and their offspring) to work conducting ornithology classes in your own backyard.

Based on an 11"-square box of 1/2" plywood, this bird house is simple enough in its fundamentals but offers the woodworker challenge in its details. Start by cutting out the seven basic panels. The sides are 10" x 10-1/2" (leaving 1/2" vent space at the top); the two roof panels each measure 11" x 12-1/4" and have one 11" edge beveled 45°; the floor is 3/4" x 10" x 10" plywood; and the front and back walls are 16-1/2" high, with double 45° miters to form the peak.

Before assembling these parts, bore the 3" entry hole in the front wall 4" below the peak. Then use a 4" hole saw to cut a disk of 1/4" plywood, and, from that, remove a 3" hole using the same pilot hole. Glue and clamp this ring to the entry hole to extend it outward. With that done, assemble all the walls and the roof, but leave the floor for later so you can still work from the inside.

All the vertical wall joints are covered with 1/4" x 3/4" outside corner molding, and the gable ends get 1/4" x 3/4" trim mitered to match. The same material goes around the eaves of the roof, but you should wait until trim elements are fitted before attaching this last bit of detail.

Starting from the bottom of the trim elements, the stairway is based on a piece of 2x lumber 2-1/4" high and 7" long. We suggest you assemble the whole thing on the bench and then attach it to the house with screws from the inside. The steps are 3/4" high and 3/4" wide. You can either mortise these or cut them by running the stock through flat and then on end. We picked up the turned porch posts at a doll house supply store and capped them with 3/8"-

thick, 1/2" wide railings made from fir. These are mighty tiny pieces to be cutting on a table saw; you might want to consider using a small hand miter box better suited to this scale of work. The posts are centered on the steps and 3/8" in on each side of the landing. From there, the final two split the distance three ways—about 1-3/32" each, on center. The door is simply a 2-1/2" x 5" piece of 1/4" plywood. Don't let the detail scare you; it's just a combination of two different densities of gray paint.

Above the door is an awning built up on a 4-1/2"-long piece of 2 x 2-1/4" mitered to a 90° point. Again, screw this block to the front of the house from the inside. Then apply the 1-3/4" x 3" roof panels. To cover the peak, we glued on a piece of molding from the doll house supply store. The collar beam is a piece of 3/8" x 3/8" stock 2" long, and the king post is the same material about 5/8" long. Exact dimensions aren't important here; just fiddle until they fit.

At the peak of the gable end is another collar beam and king post, this time from 1/2" stock to reflect the larger scale. The former is 4-1/8" long and the latter 1-1/2". Once these are secured, you can attach the rest of the 1/4" x 3/4" molding to the roof eaves.

The final bit of fanciful detail is the belfry, a 4-1/4" piece of 2 x 2 with a mitered point. 1" holes are bored through all four sides to form the cavity for the doll house bell. (It actually rings!) After you've attached the belfry, cover the remainder of the roof peak with more doll house molding.

To complete the house, set the 3/4" plywood floor in place and bore two holes through each side and into the edge of the floor with a no.8 countersink bit. No.8 x 1" screws will hold the floor in place and allow easy removal for cleaning.

Few one-room school houses remain in use these days. In fact, modern youngsters may be at a loss to figure out what this bird house is supposed to be. If so, it's time they learned.

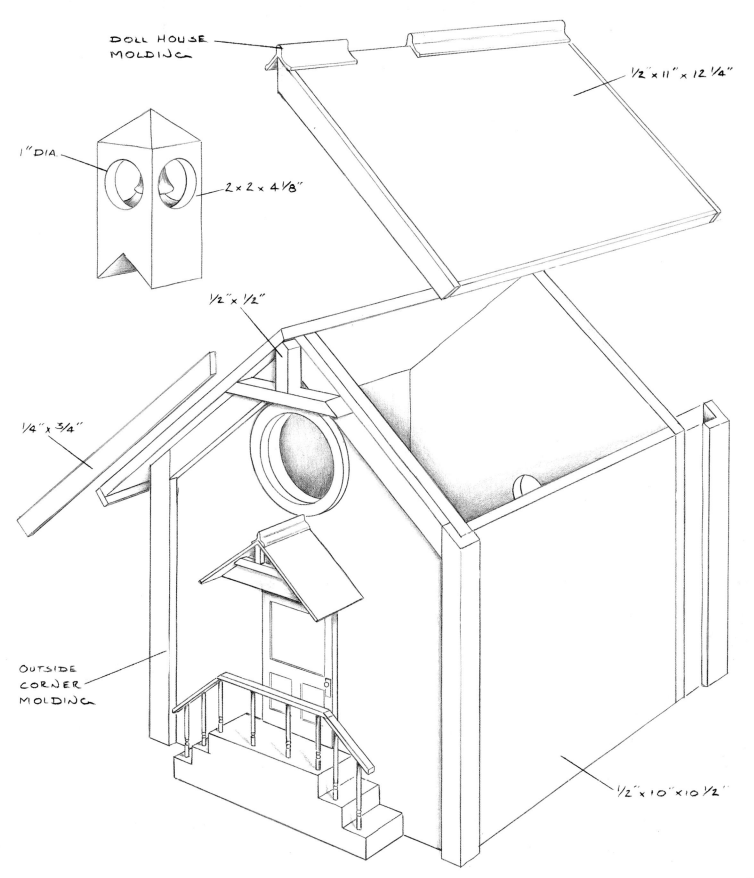

DOLL HOUSE
MOLDING

1/2" x 11" x 12 1/4"

1" DIA.

2 x 2 x 4 1/8"

1/2" x 1/2"

1/4" x 3/4"

OUTSIDE
CORNER
MOLDING

1/2" x 10" x 10 1/2"

87

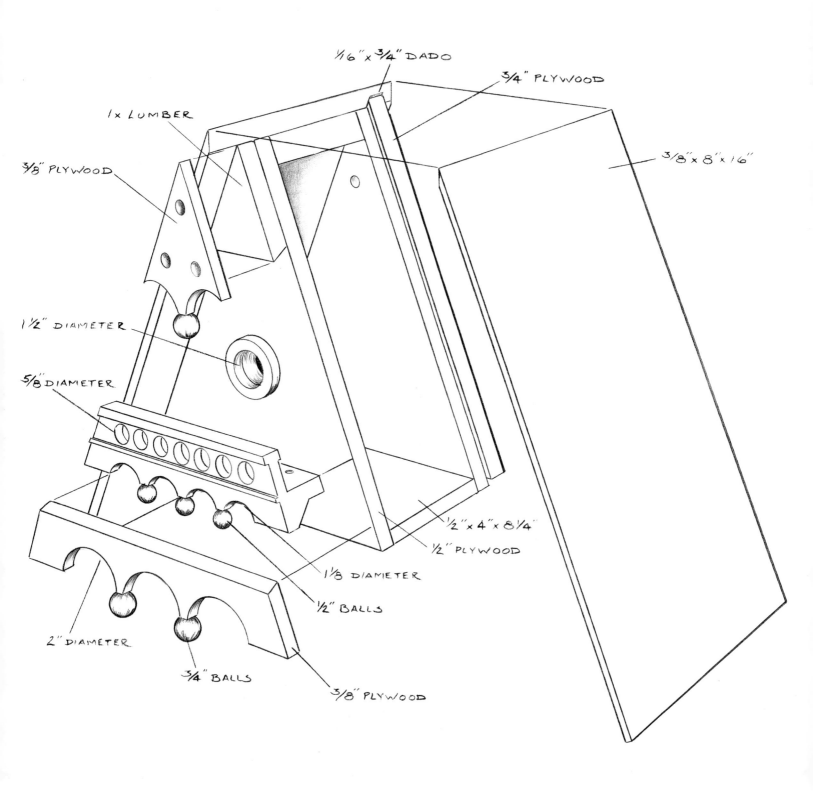

1/16" x 3/4" DADO

3/4" PLYWOOD

1x LUMBER

3/8" PLYWOOD

3/8" x 8"x16"

1 1/2" DIAMETER

5/8" DIAMETER

1/2" x 4" x 8 1/4"

1/2" PLYWOOD

1 1/8 DIAMETER

1/2" BALLS

2" DIAMETER

3/4" BALLS

3/8" PLYWOOD

Southern Mansion

Look out Scarlet, Tara's turning condo for south bound carpet-bagging martins.

One of the unanticipated benefits of preparing this book has been the architectural education we've gotten trying to mimic human residences in bird scale. The Southern Mansion, for example, turned out, when reduced to its significant elements, to be an enclosed Parthenon. Not only because of its columns, just as much for its cornice and the porch below the columns, it is clearly "Greek revival."

The core of this house is a 7-3/4"-deep, 21"-square box. The front panel overlaps the top, bottom, and sides, and has 2-1/2" holes centered 3", 8-1/4", and 15" up from the bottom and 3-3/4", 10-1/2", and 17-1/4" from the left side. Assemble the box with glue and nails, leaving out the inset back panel at this point.

Next, prepare the dormers by cutting two 16" pieces of 2 x 6 with a 45° bevel at one end. Screw the boards to each side from the inside with no.8 x 1-1/2" woodscrews so they're flush with the bottom and the back.

Form the front porch by dadoing 1/2" steps into a 2 x 4 x 21". To allow rain to drain between the steps and the house, the 2 x 4 is doweled to the 3/4" plywood so it sets out 1/16" from the front wall. Drill three 1/2" holes 1/2" deep, centered 3/8" up the front wall and equally spaced along it. Drill corresponding holes in the 2 x 4 steps; painstaking accuracy will pay off here. Then saw off three 1-1/16" lengths of 1/2" dowel, make sure the holes are thoroughly cleaned out, and glue everything together.

The column pedestals are 2"-square pieces of 1/2" plywood. Like the parthenon feeder, the columns on this house are inset 1/4" into pedestals, top and bottom. Use a spade or auger bit to bore these 1-1/4" holes, and glue and nail four of the pedestals to the porch, positioning their left sides 1/4", 6", 12-3/4", and 18-3/4" from the left edge of the porch.

At the top, the pedestals are attached to a 2 x 2-1/2" x 21" block. Cut this piece, and glue and nail the other four pedestals in locations corresponding to those below. Next, cut the four 17-3/8" closet rod columns, glue them into the pedestals in the porch, slide the upper pedestal assembly over their tops, and screw the upper block to the front wall from the inside.

To divide the interior into 6" x 6" apartments, cut four pieces of 3/4" plywood 6-1/4" wide and 19-1/2" long. Then follow the procedure for egg-crate joining described in the Cupola. This tick-tack-toe-looking assembly slides into the box from the rear and can be secured with nails through the walls, roof, and floor into its ends. A removable 3/4" x 19-1/2" x 19-1/2" sheet of plywood closes off the back.

Roof sheathing consists of a 12" x 24" piece of 1/2" plywood glued and nailed to the top of the 3/4" plywood box. Once that's in place, trim the top with mitered 1-1/4" crown molding. Repeat this process on the dormers using 3/4" base cap molding.

We suggest that you make a full-scale mockup of the copper roof in thin cardboard before you consider putting snips to metal. The multiple slopes complicate the shape before folding, and this is a fairly big piece of material (18" x 27"). In fact, you might find cutting and folding the 3" x 6-1/2" dormer roofs a confidence-building warmup to tackling the main roof. The main roof stands 4" above the sheathing at the back and has its corner creases positioned 6" in from the left and right edges horizontally (the hypotenuse of the triangle is 7"). We found that the folds make the copper stiff enough that no support is needed underneath. Nail the copper sheets to the wood below with copper brads.

The Southern Mansion is designed to be mounted to a wall. Because of its heft, though, you'll probably want to position it low enough that you don't need more than a short step-stool to reach it for removal and cleaning. We'd suggest sinking 3/8" lag screws through your home's siding and into wall studs for security. You might bore pairs of holes in the

MATERIALS LIST

3/4" x 21" x 21" Plywood
(2) 3/4" x 7" x 19-1/2" Plywood
(2) 3/4" x 7" x 21" Plywood
(2) 2 x 6 x 16" Pine
2 x 4 x 21" Pine
(3) 1/2" x 1-1/16" Dowels
(8) 1/2" x 2" x 2" Plywood
2 x 2-1/2" x 21" Pine
(4) 1-1/4" x 17-3/8" Closet rods
(4) 3/4" x 6-1/4" x 19-1/2" Plywood
3/4" x 19-1/2" x 19-1/2" Plywood
1/2" x 12" x 24" Plywood
5', 1-1/4" Crown molding
2', 3/4" Base cap molding
18" x 27" 18-22 ga. Copper sheets
(2) 3" x 6-1/2" 18-22 ga. Copper sheets
6d Galvanized finish nails
Copper brads
(12) no.8 x 1-1/2" Brass flathead woodscrews
(2) 3/8" x 3" Lag screws

Paint Pointer

The Southern Mansion is a particularly good example of how much can be done with paint. Both the front door and the windows on the dormers are lent the impression of depth by the use of multiple shades of gray paint. Darker grays form shadows that emphasize the lighter grays of the actual elements.

Southern Mansion

mansion's back wall—one large enough to pass over the lag screw's head just below a smaller one that fit's the screw's shank. That way you can remove it by just lifting a bit and pulling it away from the wall.

Though we imagine this house at the end of a long drive lined by live oaks festooned with Spanish moss, you shouldn't dismiss it just because you're a Yankee. If anyone asks, just say it's "Greek revival."

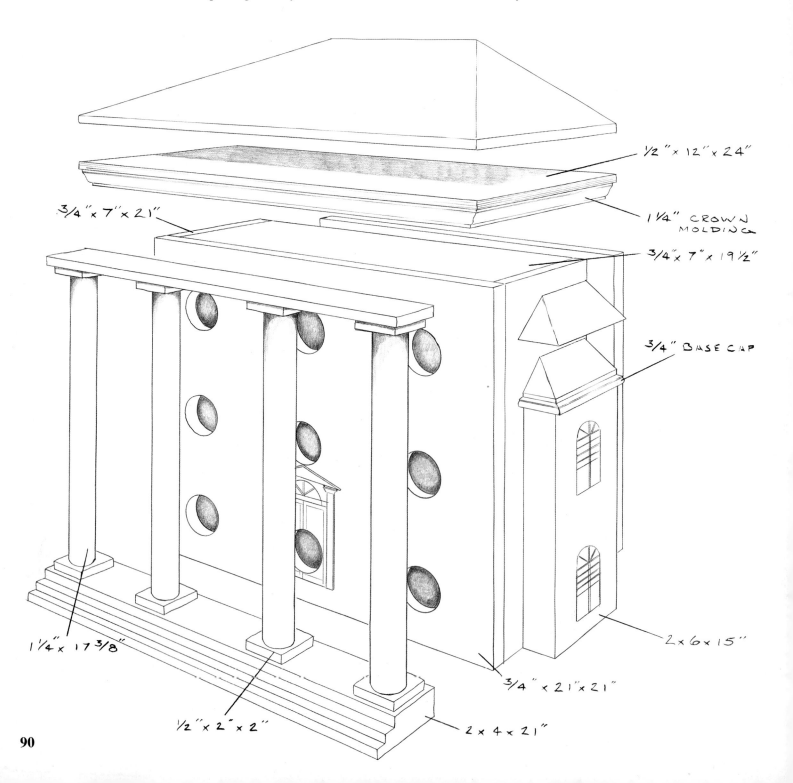

½ " x 12" x 24"

1 ¼" CROWN MOLDING

¾" x 7" x 21"

¾" x 7" x 19½"

¾" BASE CAP

1 ¼" x 17 ⅜"

2 x 6 x 15"

¾ " x 21" x 21"

½" x 2" x 2"

2 x 4 x 21"

The Haunted Bird House

The Raven

MATERIALS LIST

(4) 3/4" x 11-1/2" x 21"
   Plywood
3/4" x 11-1/2" x 11-1/2"
   Plywood
3/4" x 10" x 10" Plywood
6', 3/4" Base cap molding
2 x 4" x 7' Pine
6', 1-1/4" Picture molding
1 x 2" x 8-1/4" Pine
3-1/2" x 7-1/2" Tempered
   hardboard
(2) 8-1/4"-long Shelf edge
   molding
5"-long Shelf edge molding
(2) 1-1/4" x 1-1/4" x 2-1/2"
   Pine
(2) 1" Wooden balls
(42) 1-1/2" Wooden pegs
(2) 3/4" Wooden balls
3/16" Dowel
2 x 4" x 6-1/4" Pine
2 x 4" x 6-3/4" Pine
1 x 3-5/8" x 6" Pine
15" Doll house dental
   molding
(2) 5/8" x 8-7/8" Dowels
12" x 12" 18-22 ga. Copper
6d Galvanized finish nails
8d Galvanized finish nails
(8) no.8 x 1-1/2" Brass
   flathead woodscrews

"And the raven, never flitting, still is sitting, *still* is sitting..."-- Edgar Allen Poe

We're not sure why, but there's a bit of a sinister overtone about this bird house. Maybe it's the accentuated slope of the front stoop awning. Maybe it's the embattlements on the roof. Or maybe it's just the paint. In any event, while the look leaves us a teensy bit wary, we're confident that the sparrows aren't up on their Poe and, absent any ravens, won't object.

Beneath all the trim you'll find a basic 11-1/2"-square, 21"-high, 3/4"-plywood box with mitered corners. The top overlaps the sides, while the floor is recessed inside. At this point you can assemble all the pieces of the box except the floor.

The mansard roof is made up entirely of trim components. Starting 1/4" below the roof, we have mitered 3/4" base cap molding, followed by 2 x 4" stock beveled to leave a 1/2" thickness at the top. Depending on your table-saw's depth capacity, you may have to work from both sides of the board to achieve the 4" bevel. Prepare about 7' of this material; you'll use it in both the front and side porch roofs.

Directly below the beveled 2x lies mitered picture molding with its back against the underside of the 2x. Spaced 1" each side of the corners are 1/2"-wide sections of crown molding that serve as corbels for the picture molding eaves.

The roof over the front stoop duplicates the mansard main roof, including the 1" taper from bottom to top. Place the 2 x 4" segment before the base cap and picture molding, positioning its bottom 9-3/4" above the base and centering it left-right in the front wall.

Next, cut a 2" x 8-1/4" piece of 1x stock and bevel three of its edges 1/4" at 45°. Screw this board to the front wall from the inside with no.8 x 1-1/2" screws. The posts are 1-1/4" x 1-1/4" x 2-1/2" with bevels at the top, and verti-

cal saw kerfs for decoration. On those go 1" balls attached with 3/16" dowel. Position these posts 3/8" in from the outer corners of the porch and nail them from underneath.

The door is made from tempered hardboard and measures 3-1/2" x 7-1/2". Glue it in place and then drill the 1-1/2" entry hole centered 6-1/4" above the bottom. To frame the door, use sections of shelf edge molding. The doorknob is a tiny bead glued to the hardboard.

The lamps that brace the front entrance consist of upside-down pegs with 3/4" wooden balls. Both of these items are available at craft stores. We mounted the lamps with 1/2" sections of 3/16" dowel drilled and glued into the pegs and the wall.

To give the side porch more authority, it's cut from 2 x 4" material, with 3/4" steps. In keeping with the motif, each step is beveled 1/4" at 45°. Drill 1/4"-deep 5/8" holes for the posts at the corners, flush to the edge of the bevel. Position the side porch 2-1/4" back from the front wall, and screw it to the wall from the inside.

The roof over the side porch is a bit more complicated than the front one. Start with a 6-3/4"-long section of the beveled 2 x 4", and set your tablesaw blade to 16°. Run each of the short edges past the blade to form the additional tapers on the roof top. Now, prepare a 3-5/8" x 6" piece of 1x. Bevel three edges of one face of this board 1/4" at 45°, and bore 1/4"-deep 5/8" holes in the corners flush with the bevel. Then glue and nail it to the 2x so it's flush with the back and recessed 3/8" from the other three edges. In this recess, miter dental molding from a doll house supply shop.

Cut two 5/8" dowels, 8-7/8" long, to support the side porch roof. Glue the dowels into the holes in the porch, and fit the roof on top of them. Holding everything square, nail and glue the porch roof to the wall from the inside.

To complete the construction, glue a 12" square sheet of copper over the top of the house, and drill holes through it and into the roof to accept the 1-1/2" pegs. These holes are 1" on center, starting 1/2" in from each corner.

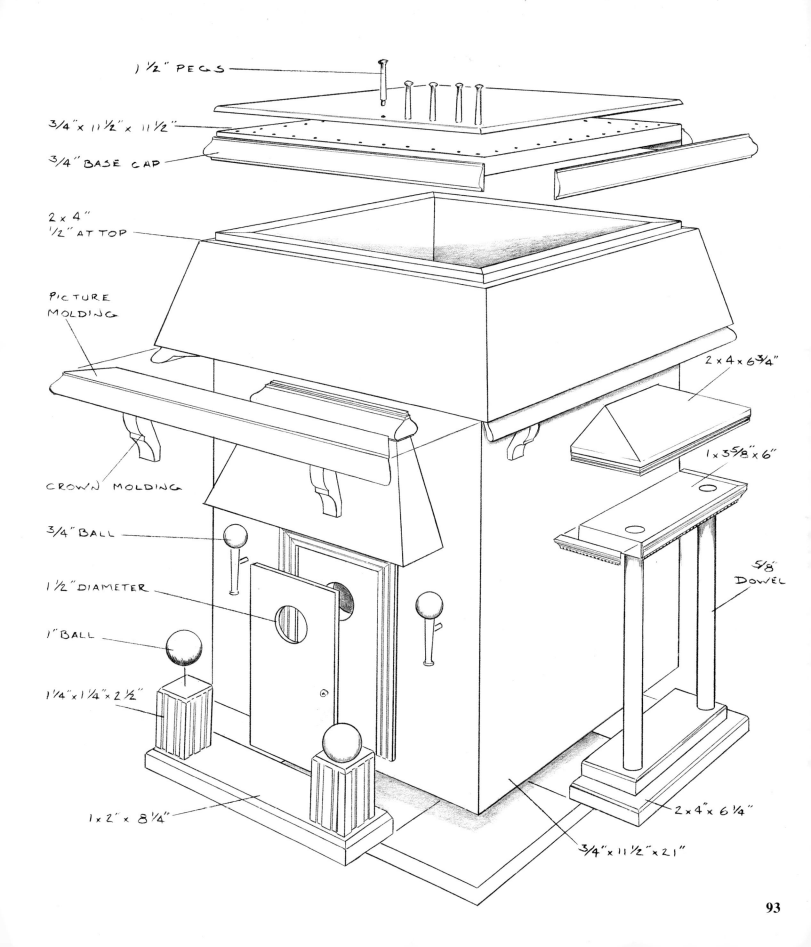

1½" PEGS

3/4" x 11½" x 11½"

3/4" BASE CAP

2 x 4"
½" AT TOP

PICTURE
MOLDING

CROWN MOLDING

3/4" BALL

1½" DIAMETER

1" BALL

1¼" x 1¼" x 2½"

1 x 2" x 8¼"

2 x 4 x 6¾"

1 x 3⅝" x 6"

5/8"
DOWEL

2 x 4" x 6¼"

3/4" x 11½" x 21"

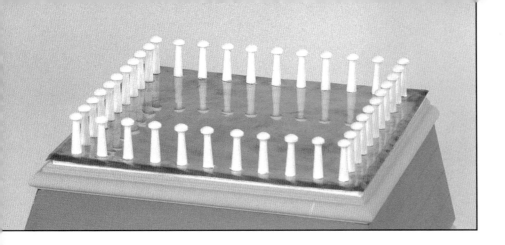

Haunted Bird House

Glue the pegs into the roof, sealing the joint with the adhesive to prevent water from seeping in. The 10" square base should be screwed into the walls so it can be removed for cleaning. Don't forget to drill a few 1/4" drainage holes in it. Sparrows forced to stand knee deep are likely to quoth the raven, "Nevermore."

Bedeviled Bevels

Cutting a perfectly smooth bevel on a tablesaw is no small trick. In fact, we can't tell you how. But we can tell you how to hide an imperfect one. Start by beveling stock that's 4-1/2" wide, instead of 4". The cut face will go against the wall of the house. Once the bevel is acceptably flat, run both edges of the stock against the blade with it set to 90º. Now the sole uncut (and factory-smooth) side will face out.

This Victorian bird house lends a special accent to interior decor.

The Golden-Crested Wren

Though it's really no more complex than the Haunted Bird House or the Colonial Townhouse, this project's small scale results in the finest detail work of any in this book. But before you flip the page in panic at the thought of trying to saw 1/16" stock on a tablesaw, remember that all the tiny components in this house are available at craft and doll-house supply stores. Thus, building a row house of your own liking is more a matter of imaginative layout and pinpoint gluing than precision saw work.

MATERIALS LIST

(4) 3/4" x 6-1/2" 10"
    Plywood
3/4" x 7" x 7" Plywood
1 x 2-1/2" x 12" Pine
1 x 1-1/2" x 2-1/2" Pine
1-1/4" x 2-3/4" Tempered
    hardboard
1/4" x 1/4" Doll house stock
1-3/16" x 2-1/4" x 2-1/2"
    Pine
2x Right isosceles triangle
    w/ 2-3/4" base
Doll house porch posts
3/16" x 1-1/2" x 2-1/2" Pine
2', 3/4" Cove molding
30", 1/4" Quarter-round
1', 3/16" Half-round
1/16" x 1" x 12" Doll house
    stock
1/4" x 1/4" x 12" Doll house
    stock
1/16" x 1/8" x 4' Doll house
    stock
1/16" x 1/16" x 3' Doll house
    stock
6d Galvanized finish nails
(10) no. 8 x 1-1/2" Brass
    flathead woodscrews

Set up especially for bluebirds, but commodious for chicadees as well, the 5" x 5" floor plan is enclosed in a mitered 6-1/2"-square, 10"-high, 3/4"-plywood cylinder. On top goes a slightly oversized 7"-square roof to help emphasize the corbeling. Pick one side as the front and bore a 1-1/2" entry hole, centered 6-3/4" up and 1-3/4" from the left edge.

To form the bay windows, rip a 2-1/2"-wide, 12"-long piece of 1x, tilt the table saw blade 30°, and bevel both edges. From this stock, cut one piece 1" long and another 10" long. Glue and nail the longer one to the front of the house, so its right edge is 3/8" in from the right wall of the house. Above it, on the 3/4" plywood roof overhang, attach the 1" segment of beveled stock.

Before tackling the detail work on the bay windows, let's work on the front porch and balcony. From the bottom, building upward, the porch is a 1-1/2" x 2-1/2" piece of 1x with 3/8" steps. Screw it to the front wall from the inside, set in 3/8" from the left wall. The front door is 1-1/4" x 2-3/4" tempered hardboard, with 7/8" squares of 1/16" doll house stock for panels. A copper nail, not quite set, does a good imitation of a door knob while helping to hold things together. Door casings are 1/4" stock, mitered at the corners.

We used turned doll house porch posts cut down to 2-3/4" to support the balcony. That part, however, is rendered from a piece of pine that started out as a 1-3/16" x 2-1/4" x 2-1/2" block. First, set the saw blade to 45° and a height of 3/4". With the rip fence set 9/16" from the base of the blade, run a 1-3/16" x 2-1/2" face through in both directions to remove a V on the underside of the balcony. Next, return to vertical, mount a 3/4" dado, set its depth to 3/4", and readjust the fence to keep it 9/16" from the cutting edge. Run the side of the stock opposite the V through in both directions to remove a total width of 1-3/8", leaving 9/16" on each side. Now, turn the stock so the V notch is up and running perpendicular to the blade, and run the wood through the saw again. Then flip it, keeping the same face against the fence, and repeat. To finish the balcony, lower the dado to a height of 1/8", and repeat the process on the front, so the square posts are revealed. Mount the finished piece 3/8" from the left wall, so its floor is 5" up.

Two more 2" posts support the triangular balcony roof. That piece is an isosceles right triangle of 2x lumber with a 2-3/4" base. Center it on the posts and run a screw in from behind. Then add the beveled 3/16" x 1-1/2" x 2-1/2" roof panels.

At this point, you can start to add trim. If you happen to have a power miter box, this would be a great time to get it out. Otherwise a hand miter box, tablesaw, or radial arm saw will do. From the top, there's 3/4" mitered cove molding attached to the edge of the roof, and then 1/4" quarter-round just below it. The other two bands that go all the way around the house are 3/4" shelf edge molding.

From here you can take the detail as far as your fancy leads you. We'll briefly describe what we've done to give you some ideas. Bear in mind that all of the following components came from a craft store, and there's even more there to choose from. The bay windows were all assembled piece-by-piece from 1/16"-thick material; the window frames are 1/8" wide, while the sashes are 1/16"; the panels above and below are 3/4" square. Mitered 1/4" quarter-round sits right above the upper windows. The sills below both are 3/16" half-round.

Entry Options

As complicated as the detail work is on this house, one has to wonder if a bird will find the way in. Consider placing the entry hole on the side or back, either of which presents a less-imposing egress.

Ornamentation on the balcony includes 1/4" quarter-round over the V, and 1/4"-square railings mitered together.

Copper protects the flat roof of our row house. This can be effectively formed in place. Cut out the shape of the roof, adding 1/4" all around. Lay it onto the roof and begin to fold the edges over. At the outside corners, slit the copper with snips so it can overlap; snip it at inside corners so it can open slightly. Once you get the copper overlapped evenly and squarely, tack the edges to the plywood with copper brads.

Because of the trim around the foundation of the house, it would be difficult to inset a floor. Therefore, we suggest you screw a base to the house from underneath, so it can be removed for cleaning. Otherwise, consider dividing the back wall in half horizontally (with a beveled cut) and screwing the lower portion in place so it can be removed. Likewise, a few ventilation holes high in the back would probably be welcomed by the occupants.

In the end, the tiny details of this house are what set it apart—they are the accomplishment. The only problem is: who wants to set this house out next to a pasture on a fencepost, far from admiring eyes?

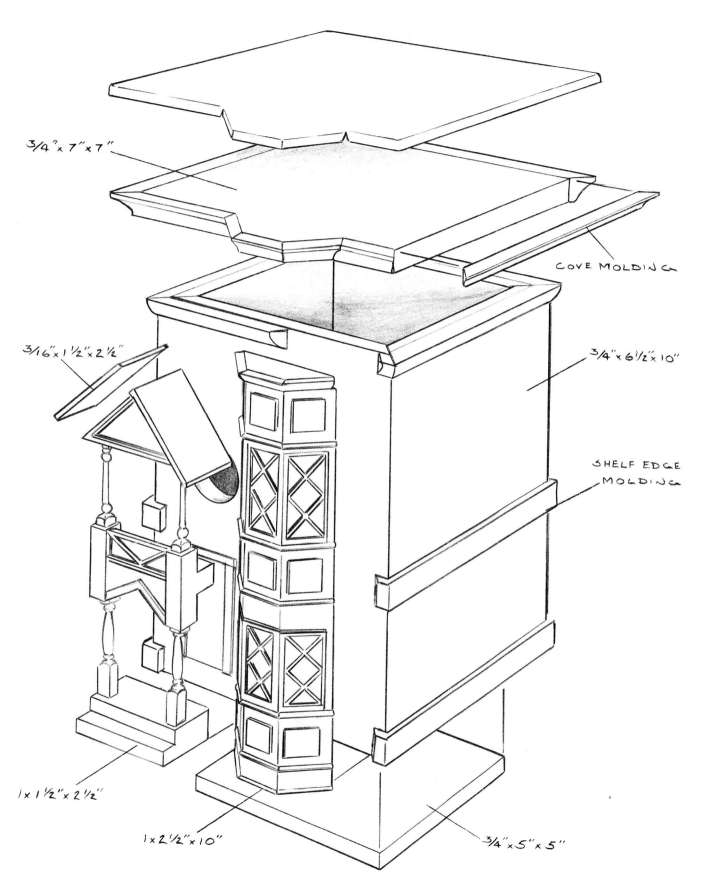

3/4" x 7" x 7"

COVE MOLDING

3/16" x 1½" x 2½"

3/4" x 6½" x 10"

SHELF EDGE
MOLDING

1 x 1½" x 2½"

1 x 2½" x 10"

3/4" x 5" x 5"

Fifties Tract Home

In the aftermath of World War II, the American dream of home ownership became a reality for many because of the suburban tract house. Simple boxes distinguished from one another mainly by variations in paint and details, the description "cookie cutter homes" was often apt. Our problem is that, to our knowledge, this is the only avian tract house in existence. Arguably, we shouldn't call it a tract house—not until you get busy and build a bevy of duplicates.

Landscaping

While unbroken lawn is certainly appropriate for the Fifties Tract Home, we were tempted to indulge ourselves at the craft store. If you haven't looked into the materials available for decorating model railroads and doll houses, you're in for a side trip through fantasy land. Don't let our austerity hold you back.

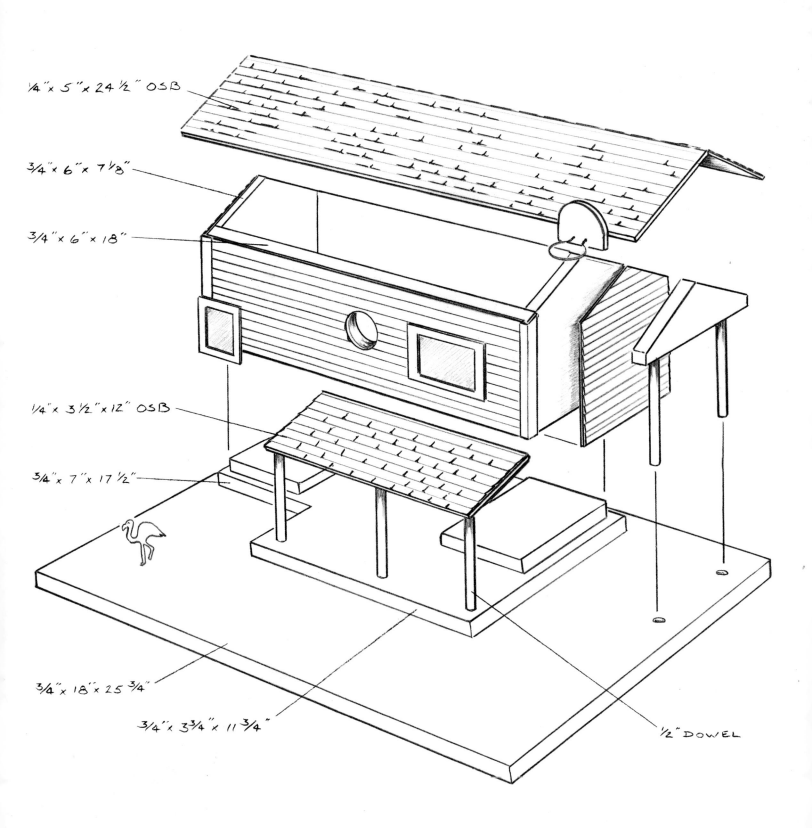

¼" x 5" x 24 ½" OSB

¾" x 6" x 7 ⅛"

¾" x 6" x 18"

¼" x 3 ½" x 12" OSB

¾" x 7" x 17 ½"

¾" x 18" x 25 ¾"

¾" x 3 ¾" x 11 ¾"

½" DOWEL

Appropriately enough, plywood is the motif for this bird house. Its base, incorporating the yard and driveway, is 3/4" x 18" x 25-3/4". Atop that goes the foundation, a 3/4" x 7" x 17-1/2" piece, and the front porch, measuring 3/4" x 3-3/4" x 11-3/4". Position the foundation about 1-1/4" in from the left rear corner of the base; the porch, of course, goes in front of and flush with the right side of the foundation.

At this point drill four or five 1/4" holes through the foundation and base in the "bedroom" for drainage. Then chuck your 1/2" bit and bore two 1/4" deep holes centered 3/4" in from each front corner of the porch, one centered 3/4" back from the front and in the middle left-right, and two more centered 1-1/2" from the right side of the base and 2" and 7-1/2" from the back. These holes will accommodate the 1/2" dowels that support the porch roof and carport.

Because the walls overlap the foundation by 1/4", it's helpful to have nailers inside. These consist of 3/4" x 5-1/4" x 6" plywood squares at each end of the house, set back from the edge of the foundation 1/2" with their long dimension front to back. The two end walls and the partitions that form the 6"-square chamber inside are 3/4" x 6" x 7-1/8" boards with the roof slope of about 20° mitered into their tops. The same angle is beveled onto the top of the 3/4" x 6" x 18" front and back walls. Attach the two end walls and the front wall to the nailers inside using 6d galvanized finish nails and glue. Affix the back wall with no.8 x 1-1/4" brass flathead woodscrews so it can be removed for cleaning.

We confess to committing an anachronism in building the roof. Oriented strand board wasn't around in the fifties, but we're convinced builders would have jumped to use it had it been available. The two roof sections measure 1/4" x 5" x 24-1/2", and are beveled to the roof slope on one long edge. While you're cutting OSB, go ahead and prepare a 3-1/2" x 12" piece for the porch roof.

To support the roof over the carport, cut a 3" x 7-1/2" gable from 3/4" plywood. Drill 1/4"-deep 1/2" holes in one long edge of this board,

centered 1-1/4" x 5-3/4" from one end. Next, miter the other side to match the roof slope. With glue, insert 1/2" x 6-1/2" dowels into the holes in the gable end and then insert the assembly into the base. To complete the roof installation, nail the OSB to the tops of the walls (not the back one) and the gable end with 4d galvanized finish nails.

The bevel lap siding comes from a doll house supply store, as does the 1/16" x 3/8" material for the corner posts. Fasteners aren't necessary with these materials; just glue them in place. Once the glue has set, go ahead and drill the 2" entry hole in the front wall 3" up from the bottom. The windows consist of a frame made from 1/16" stock enclosing unexposed pieces of black-and-white photographic film. These may not prove to be durable over time, but hardier substitutes are available at the doll house supply.

To support the porch roof, cut three 1/2" x 5-1/4" dowels and glue them into the holes in the porch floor. Then tack the porch roof to the tops of the posts and to the wall of the house from the inside. Only a small slope is called for here. We covered our house's roofs with doll house asphalt shingles. They come in rolls, so they're not quite as tedious to install as they might first look.

The rest of the ornamentation pretty much speaks for itself. Perhaps you'd prefer plastic deer to the flamingos. A tiny bird bath would add an ironic touch. Colors, too, are a matter of whim. Just remember, we've got the only robin's egg blue house on the block.

MATERIALS LIST

3/4" x 18" x 5-3/4" Plywood
3/4" x 7" x 17-1/2" Plywood
3/4" x 3-3/4" x 11-3/4" Plywood
(2) 3/4" x 5-1/4" x 6" Plywood
(4) 3/4" x 6" x 7-1/8" Plywood
(2) 3/4" x 6" x 18" Plywood
(2) 1/4" x 5" x 24-1/2" OSB
1/4" x 3-1/2" x 12" OSB
3/4" x 3" x 7-1/2" Plywood
(2) 1/2" x 6-1/2" Dowels
Doll house siding
Doll house trim
Doll house shingles
Assorted knickknacks
6d Galvanized finish nails
4d Galvanized finish nails
(4) no.8 x 1-1/4" Brass flathead woodscrews

The Goldfinch

A phosphorescent strip tacked to the eaves creates a neon effect at dusk.

Fly-by-Night Motel

Since it lacks a heated pool or waterbeds, the automobile association might rate our motel as only a one-star accommodation. But we think passing purple martins will find the fly-up convenience hard to resist. Who knows, they may even ask for weekly rates. Offering neighborly yet decently private housing for these most congenial nesting birds, this 50s-era, mom-and-pop flytel will liven up your yard, as will its occupants.

MATERIALS LIST

(2) 3/4" x 6" X 7" X 7-1/2"
   Plywood
(5) 3/4" x 6" x 6-1/4" x
   6-3/4" Plywood
3/4" x 6-3/4" x 21" Plywood
3/4" x 6-3/4" x 27-3/4"
   Plywood
3/4" x 7-5/8" x 14-1/4"
   Plywood
3/4" x 7-5/8" x 21" Plywood
3/4" x 6" x 19-1/2" x 26-1/4"
   Plywood

The house is basically an L-shaped 3/4" plywood box with ornamentation. The only complication is the roof slope, which requires bevel and miter cuts of about 5°. The simplest approach here is to cut the end and partition walls first, and then trim the front and back walls to fit. Prepare two end walls and five partitions. The end walls measure 6" on the base, 7" on one vertical, and 7-1/2" on the other, while the partitions are 3/4" shorter (6" x 6-1/4" x 6-3/4") to butt against the base.

Next, cut out a 4'2" length of 3/4" ply 6-3/4" wide, with a 5° bevel along one edge. Then, set the saw blade back to square and rip off a 3' length about 7-5/8" wide (leaving the 5°

bevel from the last cut on one edge). Now check the short face of the front wall and the tall face of the back wall against an end wall to see that the bevels and miter cuts all match up perfectly. Trim until they do. Once they're just the right size, crosscut the back wall with the blade set at 45° to form pieces 21" and 27-3/4" long, and the front wall at the same bevel to form pieces 14-1/4" and 21" long. The bevel cuts form miter joints at the corners.

Now drill the 2-1/2" entry holes in the front walls at points centered 3" from the bottom, and 4" and 10-1/2" from the outer end of the short section, then 2-1/2", 10-1/2", and 17" from the outer end of the long section. At this point, you could also add an entry hole in back

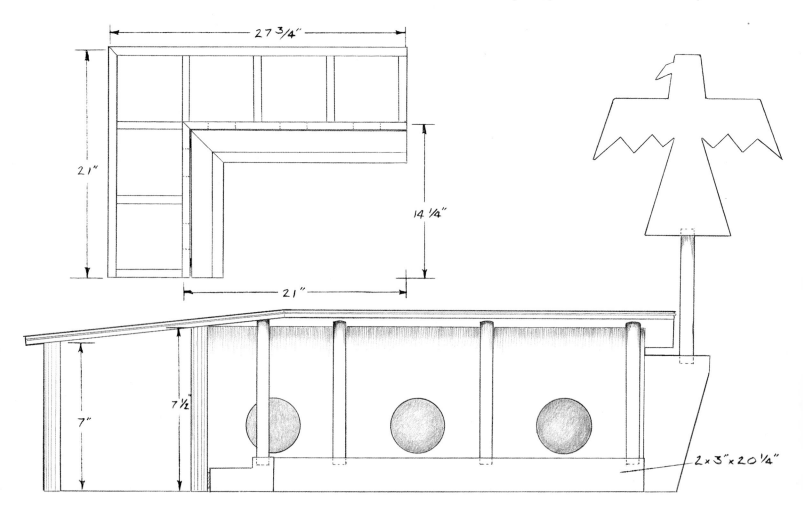

27 3/4"

21"

14 1/4"

21"

7 1/2"

7"

2 x 3" x 20 1/4"

to access the "room" at the corner. (Perhaps it can be the manager's quarters.)

The sidewalk is cut from 2x fir 3" wide, with a 1/2" x 2" chunk removed from the top. Prepare about 3'6" of the material and then cut one piece 13-1/2" long and another 20-1/4" long, mitered so they meet at the inside corner. Place shims about 1/16" thick every 6" or so between the walkways and the front walls before you nail them from the inside with 8d galvanized finish nails. The gap will allow water to drain through, rather than pooling.

One more piece needs to be attached before assembling the walls of the house. The standard for the sign is a 6" length of the same 2 x 3" stock used for the walkway. We tapered it to 1-1/2" width at the bottom, starting about an inch below the top. Attach the standard from the inside of the end wall using two no.8 x 1-1/2" brass flathead woodscrews.

The base of the bird house is a 6" x 19-1/2" x 26-1/4" L of 3/4" plywood that fits inside all the exterior walls. Once you've cut it out, you can assemble the walls and partitions around and atop it with glue and 6d nails. Don't, however, attach the base to the walls and partitions permanently. Countersink no.8 x 1-1/2" woodscrews at strategic points so the base can be removed for cleaning.

Two roof panels from 1/4" oriented strand board are needed to accommodate the twin roof slopes. Both are 12" wide; one is 23" long, the other 30". Miter one end of each at 45° so they can meet. Before you secure the roof, cut five 6-1/2" posts from 5/8" dowel, mitering one end at 5° to match the roof slope. Cut the heads off five 4d finish nails and push the cut off ends into the square ends of the dowels. Apply glue sparingly to ends with the nails and space them evenly along the walkway, pushing the nails into the walkway to hold the dowels while the glue sets. Go ahead and position the roof panels, leaving 1/2" overhang at the back, and tack them to the walls and the dowels with 4d galvanized finished nails. Plain-old black roll roofing makes a suitable and effective cover for this 50s throwback.

All that's left is the sign itself. Refer to the diagram and your own creativity to shape a 6" or 8" piece of 2 x 6 fir into the appropriate caricature. Anyone who's been around more than a couple of decades and has traveled must have their own renditions of the thunderbird imprinted in memory. For the birds, though, this combination of pigeon perch and predator ought to be a whole new treat.

2 x 3" x 13-1/2" Fir
2 x 3" x 20-1/4" Fir
2 x 3" x 6" Fir
1/4" x 12" x 23" OSB
1/4" x 12" x 30" OSB
(6) 5/8" x 6-1/2" Dowels
Roll roofing
2 x 6 x 6" Fir
8d Galvanzied finish nails
6d Galvanized finish nails
4d Galvanized finish nails
no. 8 x 1-1/2" Brass flathead
   woodscrews

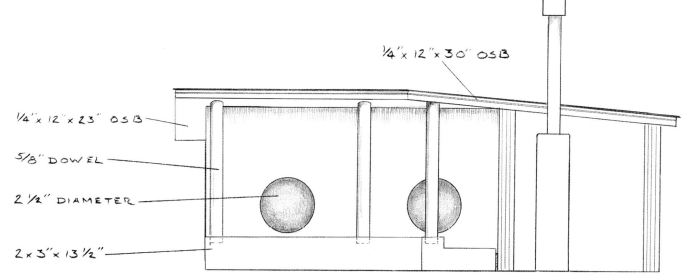

¼" x 12" x 30" OSB

¼" x 12" x 23" OSB

⅝" DOWEL

2 ½" DIAMETER

2 x 3" x 13 ½"

MATERIALS LIST

(2) 3/4" X 7-1/2" X 16"
   Plywood
(2) 3/4" x 5-1/4" x 16"
   Plywood
3/4" x 6" x 7-1/2" Plywood
2 x 10-1/2" x 10-1/2" Pine
(2) 1/2" x 8-1/2" x 8-1/2"
   Plywood
1" x 7" Dowel
1" x 3-1/4" Dowel
(2) 1 x 1-3/4" x 1-3/4" Pine
(18) Button screw hole plugs
(2) no.6 x 1-1/4" Brass
   flathead woodscrews
14" x 16" 18-22 ga. Copper
   sheet
Copper brads

*"Keep a green tree in
your heart and perhaps
the singing bird will
come."—anonymous
Chinese proverb*

Postmodern Dwelling

While there may not be a distinctly "modern" period in bird house architecture to react to, we still think this rendition earns its title by setting aside the tedious functionalism common to most bird house designs. Equally well suited to pileated woodpeckers or (with the addition of an interior ramp) wood ducks, this house is, at the least, postboring.

The Postmodern is one of the easiest projects in this book, consisting of a 16"-high box of 3/4" plywood, a top and bottom, and some ornamentation. Start by cutting the 5-1/4" sides and the 7-1/2"-wide front and back. Then cut out another piece of 3/4" plywood 6" x 7-1/2".

Fit your drill with a 4" hole saw and bore holes in the 6" x 2-1/2" and one 5-1/4" x 7-1/2" panel at points centered 4" down from the tops. Then remove 2" from the 6" board to leave a semicircle. Nail the box together, butting the 5-1/4" walls into the 7-1/2" ones, and nail the 4" board to the front so its semicircle conforms to the 4" hole.

The base is a piece of 2 x 12 bevel cut at 45° to yield a 10-1/2" square. Cut another piece of 2x to form a 5-1/4" square and nail it in the center of the smaller face of the 10-1/2" piece. This board will slide inside the bottom of the house, and screws will allow it to be removed for cleaning.

Up top go two 8-1/2" squares of 1/2" plywood, again bevel cut to 45°. Nail one to the top of the walls with its bevels down, and then top it with the other, bevels up. The copper pyramid roof can be tacked to the upper piece of plywood with copper brads.

The remainder of the house's trim consists of some 1" dowel ripped in half, two 1 x 1-3/4" x 1-3/4" blocks, and button screw hole plugs. Position the half dowels 3/8" in from the edge, so they'll be centered in the 1-3/4" rectangular trim. Attach the two square blocks with no.6 x 1-1/4" brass flathead woodscrews, and cover them with the plugs.

Drill shallow holes to fit the remainder of the decorative button screw hole plugs. Center the outside ones 7/8" in from the edge. The inner two divide the distance between the outer two into three equal parts—about 1-29/32" as it happens.

When it comes to paint, this design begs for bright colors. However, recognizing that bird taste—and particularly that of wood ducks and pileated woodpeckers—may be at variance with our own, we went pastel. Likely enough, though, like humans, given a little time, they'll adapt to new styles.

The Pied Woodpecker

Log Suet Feeder

There's very little to this feeder, yet birds seem to find it more appealing than the metal and plastic pavilions we so often offer them. Is it any wonder?

Choose a 6"- to 8"-diameter log, a foot or two in length, and bore some 1-2" holes in it with an auger or spade bit. Below each large hole, drill a smaller one to accept a dowel perch. (If you keep the perch close to the suet hole, it will at least make things more difficult for starlings.) Add an eye screw to the top for hanging, then hang it up, insert suet mixed with bird seed in the holes, and you're done.

The Reed Warbler

BIRD FEEDERS

Bark-Faced Feeder

Slab wood from the sawmill lends itself to a variety of fowl interpretations—elsewhere as a cozy wren house, here as an open feeder. Not only is it inexpensive, it blends into the landscape leaving its customers center stage.

Refer to the bark-faced house on page 42 for general suggestions on working with bark-faced wood slabs. In this case, you should also be careful to allow water to drain between the sides and platform of the feeder by placing shims between them before assembly. The roof will provide some protection from the elements, but proper drainage will do much more to help prevent warpage.

The Picnic Pagoda

MATERIALS LIST

- (2) 1 x 12 x 22" Western red cedar
- 1 x 12 x 18" Western red cedar
- 1 x 2-1/2" x 19-1/2" Western red cedar
- 1 x 2" x 11-1/4" Western red cedar
- (3) 1 x 2" x 21" Western red cedar
- (2) 1 x 3-1/2" x 14" Western red cedar
- (2) 1 x 2" x 14" Western red cedar
- (12) no.8 x 1-1/4" Brass flathead woodscrews
- Button screw hole plugs
- 8d Galvanized finish nails

East is East and West is West . . . and what better place for them to meet than in the generous and contemplative art of bird watching? Most birds, after all, are no respecters of national borders; their country is the skies, and their summer and winter homes are commonly nations apart. So bring a little of the Far East into your Western yard, and invite these feathered aeronauts to rest and dine in your pagoda feeder.

Purity and simplicity are the key words in this pagoda design, where they're combined to create a surprising elegance. Following those mandates, this feeder takes its grace from minimalism and from the beauty of unfinished cedar stock.

The Lark

The roof panels are cut from 1 x 12, each being 22" long and beveled to 45° along one long edge. The tray is an 18" length of 1 x 12, surrounded by two 1 x 2-1/2" x 19-1/2" sides, each with a decorative 30° bevel along one edge, and two ends, also cut from 1x stock, measuring 2" x 11-1/4".

The roof and base are connected by an assembly consisting of a ridge pole (1 x 2" x 21", with one long edge double-beveled to a 90° peak); two side supports (each 1 x 2" x 21", with a 45° bevel on one long edge to meet the roof); and two main poles (each 1 x 3-1/2" x 14", with a 3/4" x 2"-deep notch centered in a 90° point on one end to receive the ridge pole. To cut this end, first draw the 45° lines that form the peak with a tri-square. Then set the saw blade to a 2" height and mortise the notch. Finish by following the pencil lines to form a 90° peak with two 45° miters. A pair of cross braces (freehand the curves on one 2" x 14" strip of 1x; then cut it out, trace it onto another board, and cut a second to match) have 1/4"- deep by 3/4" mortises at points 1" in from the ends of the unscrolled edges to receive the roof supports.

To assemble the feeder, hold each tray end in position on the base and scribe a line. Then center the main poles along these lines and secure them with no.8 x 1-1/4" brass flathead wood screws. Now fasten the tray ends to the base with 8d galvanized finish nails. Next, center the ridgepole in the notches in the two uprights and fasten the roof sides to the main post with more 8d nails. With that done, center the side supports in the mortises of the cross braces, and screw them on. Finally, slip that assembly up until it meets the roof and is centered. Then drill and countersink before joining the cross braces to the poles with no.8 x 1-1/4" screws and plugging the countersinks with button plugs. (At this point, you may want to add a few more 8d nails to further secure the roof.)

Enjoy the visitors who seek the solace of your pagoda, and be sure to keep it well supplied all year for those that decide to stay. Many of your guests will, however, refresh themselves and then travel on. Wish them "sayonara" when they go.

The Jack-Daw

During planning and construction, everyone referred to this feeder as "the Frank Lloyd Wright," all the while recognizing that there's really no such thing as a generic Wright building. America's greatest architect never repeated himself, nor was he derivative. Nonetheless, this project shows heavy Wright influence. The overlapped horizontal members are reminiscent of Falling Water, while the angled roof is more characteristic of his Prairie Style. The emphasis of natural materials is a hallmark in most Wright structures, making this one of our favorites.

MATERIALS LIST

4 x 4 x 10" Salt-treated
pine
2 x 10-1/2" x 14" Clear
all-heart redwood
2 x 10-1/2" x 7" Clear
all-heart redwood
2 x 2-5/8" x 3-5/8" Clear
all-heart redwood
2 x 3-1/2" x 4-7/8" Clear
all-heart redwood
1" x 10-1/2"" x 25-1/4"
Clear all-heart redwood
(16) no.10 x 2-1/4" Brass
flathead woodscrews

This is the sole example in this book where variable mounting is not an option. The 4 x 4 post is an integral part of the structure—just as Mr. Wright would have wanted it. You'll need at least a 10-footer to keep the terrace out of kitty reach once you've buried 18" of the post in the ground, and a predator barrier will be required.

We've also cut loose and splurged on this project: other than the post, which is pressure-treated pine, all the wood is quarter-sawn clear all-heart redwood. Expensive, admittedly, but the visual interplay of the wood's color and grain with the planar design is what makes it work. Feel free to substitute a less-expensive species if you find yourself balking in the checkout line at the lumberyard, but do look for a board with the straightest, most vertical grain possible. Otherwise, warpage is likely.

To simplify the following construction description, let's talk about the feeder from one angle. Imagine that you're looking at it from the side, so that the long deck projects straight out to the left. Start by cutting the top of the post to a 75° angle (the point will be to the right), and then dado two 1-5/8"-deep grooves just shy of 1-1/2" wide across it—one on the right side with its upper edge 3-1/4" from the top, and the other on the left starting 7" down. Decks of 2 x 10-1/2" redwood slide into these dados, with slots cut just wide enough to offer a tight fit without need for pounding.

The lower (left) deck is 14" long and is offset toward you 1", leaving 4" on your side and 3" on the back. The upper deck measures 7" and is offset just the opposite—3" on your side, 4" in back. A 3-5/8" isosceles right triangle cut from 2x stock and screwed to the deck and the post supports the upper deck, while a 4-7/8" isosceles right triangle supports the lower one.

Our feeder's roof is a 1" x 10-1/2" x 25-1/4" piece of redwood. This thickness would normally be called four quarters (4/4) and may not be readily available in your locale. In that case, a 1x board (about 3/4" thick) would make a suitable substitute. The roof rests on the top of the post with 6" projecting to the right of the post and a 1" offset to the front (to be directly above the larger deck). Don't fasten this board to the post yet.

Two columns help support the roof, both cut 5" long from 2 x 4 redwood, with a 75° angle on one end. Position these boards an inch in from the edge of the deck and slide them away (or toward) the post so that the roof fits flush to their tops and that of the post. Now secure the roof and columns to the deck and post with brass screws.

Redwood is exceedingly durable, so preservatives really aren't necessary for this feeder. If you're very fond of the unweathered redwood color, a clear, water-repellant coating would be acceptable. Otherwise, the wood should be left to change with its environment—in process with its clientele.

A Seedy Eatery

Back in the days before the golden arches, small, family-owned roadside diners dotted the landscape, offering culinary adventure (and even risk!) to the traveler or vacationer. You can still find a few of these gems, of course, serving (depending upon their location) fried chicken, barbecue, fish and chips, or the ubiquitous burgers and hot dogs. We're afraid that dining dangerously in places like Joe's is an endangered pastime. So, in tribute to the perfect pieces of pie (as well as the horrible cases of heartburn) of the past, we've designed this blue-highway beanery to cater to the weary travelers along your local migration route.

All of the major components are cut from 1x lumber. The roof front measures 9" x 10", and its back 4-5/8" x 10", both beveled to 40° along one edge to meet at the peak. Two false walls fit inside the roof—each measuring 3" x 5" with one end mitered to form an 80° peak—to allow it to be securely slipped atop the walls without fasteners.

The diner's right and left sides measure 6-3/8" x 9", and are each mitered to the same 80° peak used on the roof supports. The front, which rides up allowing seed to spill beneath its lower edge, is a 6-3/8" x 9" board, beveled to 40° at one end to match the slope of the roof. The back, also beveled to the roof's pitch along one long side, measures 7-1/4" x 8-1/8".

An interior ramp funnels seed down into the dining area. It measures 5" x 8-1/8" and is beveled to 45° at each long end. The floor of the diner, which overlaps the base and will actually receive the seed, is an 8-1/8" x 8-1/8" square. Its dining area is enclosed by a railing consisting of two 1-1/2" x 2-1/2" side walls and a 1-1/2" x 9-1/2" front piece. The pillars, which will be glued into the front corners of the railing, are each 1 x 3/4" x 5-1/2", beveled to 40° at the top to support the front of the roof.

And how about a pair of outdoor tables for fair-weather fowl? Simply cut two discs from 1/4" plywood, using a 2-1/2" hole saw. Bore 1/4"-diameter holes, centered and 1/8" deep in each, and matching 1/4"-deep holes in the appropriate positions on the base. Then glue 2" lengths of 1/4" dowel in each disc, and glue the assemblies into the base.

Attach the interior supports to the roof with glue and 6d galvanized finish nails. Then do the same with the base/diner unit, gluing the seed ramp down after the walls, base, and floor are together. Remember, the roof should simply slip onto the walls, so it can be removed to add seed as needed.

The paint scheme is, of course, up to you. We suggest, though, that you take to the byways (or to the back roads of your memory) and pick out a particular ptomaine palace to commemorate. And don't expect big tips from your customers, they're likely to be cheep and ask that the meals be put on their bills.

MATERIALS LIST

1 x 9" x 10" Pine
1 x 4-5/8" x 9" Pine
(2) 1 x 3" x 5" Pine
(3) 1 x 6-3/8" x 9" Pine
1 x 7-1/4" x 8-1/8" Pine
1 x 5" x 8-1/8" Pine
1 x 8-1/8" x 8-1/8" Pine
(2) 1 x 1-1/2" x 2-1/2" Pine
1 x 1-1/2" x 9-1/2" Pine
1 x 3/4" x 9-1/2" Pine
(2) 1/4" x 2-1/2"-diameter Plywood
(2) 1/4" x 2" Dowels
6d Galvanized finish nails

The Buzzard

The Gazebo

Designed to complement our Southern Mansion bird house, the gazebo bird feeder is fairly simple to construct but quite dramatic visually. It also happens to be a case where our anthropomorphic indulgence works out particularly well for the birds.

MATERIALS LIST

1/2" x 9" x 2' OSB
1/2" x 5-3/4" x 9" Plywood
3/4" x 10-1/8" x 10-1/8"
    Plywood
3/4" x 11-1/2" x 11-1/2"
    Plywood
Chair caning
1/4" x 1/2" x 5' Pine
Assorted doll house porch
    posts
Body putty
Fiberglass roving
6d Galvanized finish nails

The hexagonally peaked roof is, in appearance at least, the most imposing component of the structure. But, thanks to the use of a few construction short cuts, it needn't give you nightmares. Begin with a 2' (or slightly longer) piece of 9"-wide 1/2" oriented strand board (or 1/2" plywood.) Set your miter gauge to 22-1/2°, and cut a right triangle off one end. Now flop the board, and make another 22-1/2° cut to produce an isosceles triangle with a base of 7-1/2" and a height of 9". Go on, flopping and turning the wood as necessary, to produce five more identical triangles.

Here's the short cut: Normally, each of these would have to be beveled if they were to fit together to create a roof. We've avoided that problem by joining the square-cut panels with body putty reinforced with fiberglass roving. Happily, the putty has a gray color when it sets that resembles a slate roof. (Another tip: You might want to make a hexagonal collar of scrap wood to hold the roof in "peak" form while it dries.)

The arched walls incorporate a trick of their own. Each is simply a 1/2" x 5-3/4" x 9" plank with its long edges bevel-cut to 30°. Then a 4"-diameter hole saw is used to bore an opening 3-3/4", on center, from one end. Straight cuts tangent to the hole and parallel to the sides proceeding to the base complete the archway.

The hexagonal floor, cut from 3/4" plywood, measures 5-1/2" on a side and 10-1/8" across. The base, upon which the floor sits, is another 3/4" plywood hexagon, but with 6-1/2" sides, that measures 11-1/2" across. It's probably best to draw these first, then set your miter gauge to 30°, and cut along the markings.

The walls, floor, and base can be assembled with construction adhesive and sparing use of 6d galvanized finish nails. Once the basic structure is together, you might want to add some ornamentation. To form railings, we cut out pieces of chair caning and glued them into a sandwich of 1/4" X 1/2" wood rails. On top, we whittled and sanded a combination of turned doll house porch posts and a wooden bead to form a spire.

Painting this feeder, except for the chair caning, is better left to last. We chose a simple white to match our Southern Mansion bird house, and left the slate-toned body putty as is. The roof is probably heavy enough to stay put if simply set in place, but it can be secured with two 2" lengths of plumber's perforated pipe-hanging strap, secured to the walls and the underside of the roof with brass flathead wood screws, if you want the extra protection against strong winds.

Fill it with the appropriate seed, and you might get to see goldfinches grazing in a gazebo. Gee.

The Magpie

A Plywood Parthenon

Modeled after one of the first, great Doric temples, our Parthenon bird feeder draws its beauty from the classic simplicity of its lines. And, while it's not exactly a beginner's level woodworking project, you'll find that many of its components are disarmingly easy to shape and assemble. Just approach the job with the proper attitude. And, to paraphrase Pallas Athena, Greek goddess of wisdom and patroness of the original Parthenon, always "measure twice and saw once."

To begin, cut the base and ceiling from 3/4" plywood; the former will measure 15-1/2" x 21-1/2", the latter 14-1/2" x 20-1/2" with an access hole cut in its center with a 6" hole saw. Now cut the 1x stock that will eventually form the upper and lower sockets for the columns. You'll need four strips measuring 2" x 21" and four more of 2" x 15".

The next step is a bit tricky. Your aim will be to shape 1-1/2" square pillar pedestals along these strips. To do so, first set your table saw for a depth of 1/4" and crosscut multiple dadoes, removing 1-1/2" to leave 1-1/2" blocks at 1-1/2" intervals along the strips. Next, rip the edge of each piece of stock with your rip fence set to remove 1/4" in width and the blade height set to remove 1/4" in depth. The result will be a series of 1/4"-high blocks. each 1-1/2" square, spaced evenly along the lengths of stock.

With that done, take a break from the tricky stuff by cutting 20 columns from 1" dowel, each measuring 7-1/2" long.

The roof assembly is next. Its base is a 15-1/2" x 21-1/2" sheet of 1/4" tempered hardboard. When this is cut, center it on the 3/4"-plywood ceiling, clamp it in position, and bore four evenly spaced 1/2" diameter holes, each 3/4" deep, to accept the dowel plugs that will hold the roof in place. (If you like, you can glue the 1" long dowel segments into the ceiling at this time . . . the roof base will slip over them later.)

The roof panels consist of two 21-1/2" x 9-1/4" sheets of 1/4" tempered hardboard. When you make your long cuts, tilt the table saw blade to about 18° and rip one long edge on each piece, then spin them around and rip the remaining long sides to produce the beveled, parallel edges that will form the roof peak and the eaves.

Marginal Material

In this and a few other projects in this book, we've used tempered hardboard for structural elements. Sharp-eyed readers will note that it was not recommended in the chapter on materials. Truth be told, we'd like to have used something more durable, but plywood, which is thicker, would have looked wrong. Tempered hardboard is rated for moist applications, but we still encourage you to keep it well protected with paint.

A Plywood Parthenon

MATERIALS LIST

3/4" x 14-1/2" x 20-1/2"
    Plywood
3/4" x 15-1/2" x 21-1/2"
    Plywood
(2) 3/4" x 4" x 20" Plywood
(4) 1 x 2" x 15" Pine
(4) 1 X 2" x 21" Pine
(20) 1" x 7-1/2" Dowels
(4) 1/2" x 1" Dowels
1/4" x 15-1/2" x 21-1/2"
    Tempered hardboard
(2) 1/4" x 9-1/4" x 21-1/2"
    Tempered hardboard
6d Galvanized nails

The roof gables are cut from 3/4" plywood. To shape them, start with two pieces, each about 20" long by about 4" wide. Lay one piece on your table saw, and adjust it so that the saw blade will form an 18° rip cut. Then tack a piece of rectangular scrap to the close end so that scrap will slide against the rip fence maintaining the 18° angle. (Be sure to hammer your nails into the scrap at a location where the blade will miss them.) Run the gable through the saw, then use the waste from that cut to serve as a guide to form the second cut that completes the peak. Repeat to shape the rear gable. (This sounds more difficult than it is, but you might want to experiment on some scrap lumber before you cut the good stuff!)

Now miter the ends of the upper and lower pedestal strips to produce two equal-sized picture frames, with those raised blocks that are halved by the miter cuts meeting at each joint to form new pedestals. Fasten these frames, centered, to the base and roof with glue and 6d galvanized nails. Then, using a pencil and a straight edge, mark diagonals on each raised pedestal to determine the center point, and drill 1"-diameter holes, to a depth of 1/4", into the center of each one. (If you've got a drill press, it'll make this job easier.) With that done, change bits and drill one 3/8" hole in each corner of the base, just inside the pedestal frame, for drainage.

Now you can glue the roof assembly together, taking special care to get a good seal at the peak. (We didn't use any hardware here, but 6d galvanized nails, run through the roof and into the 3/4" plywood gables, would certainly help hold everything more securely.)

When the roof assembly has dried thoroughly, you'll probably want to paint all of the components before fitting them together. A flat white latex is a good choice and is really all that's needed to produce a striking feeder. You might, however, want to go the extra mile and use a fine brush and gray paint to flute the pillars and add some fanciful heroic carvings on the gable ends as we did. Then, just slip the Parthenon together. It's really quite sturdy as is, though you might want to use glue on the column tops and bottoms to be safe. (Don't, however, glue the ceiling dowels into the roof. You'll need access to the 6" hole to fill and clean the feeder.)

Admittedly, our Parthenon feeder isn't a single afternoon's project, but it'll amply reward the time you spend building it. After all, you simply have to add some millet and sunflower seeds and you'll have a veritable Greek chorus in your own backyard!

The Long-Eared Owl

122

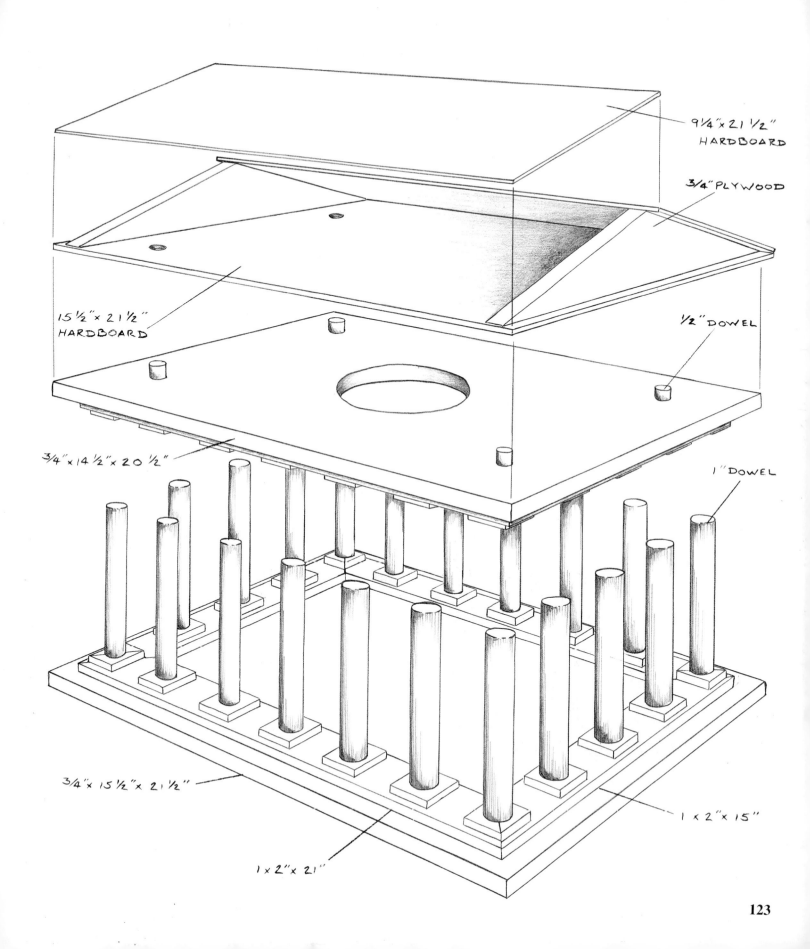

9¼" x 21 ½"
HARDBOARD

3/4" PLYWOOD

15 ½" x 21 ½"
HARDBOARD

½" DOWEL

3/4" x 14 ½" x 20 ½"

1" DOWEL

3/4" x 15 ½" x 21 ½"

1 x 2" x 15"

1 x 2" x 21"

123

A Versatile Mix: White proso millet, fine cracked corn, and black oil sunflower (see birds for the next three listings)

White Proso Millet: Cardinals, Cowbirds, Finches (House, Chaffinch, Green Finch), Mourning Doves, Redpolls (Common), Sparrows (Field, House, White-throated), Wrens (Carolina)

Fine Cracked Corn: Blue Jays, Cardinals, Grosbeaks (Evening and Rose-Breasted), Sparrows (Field, House, and others), Towhees (Green-tailed, Spotted, and Rufous-sided)

Black Oil Sunflower: American Goldfinches, Cardinals, Chickadees (Black-capped and Carolina), Grosbeaks (Evening and Rose-breasted), Grackles (Common), Finches (House and Purple), Mourning Doves, Sparrows (Field, House, Chipping, and White-throated)

Black Striped Sunflower: Blue Jays, Cardinals, Chickadees (Black-capped and Carolina), Grosbeaks (Evening and Red-breasted), Grackles (Common), Finches (House and Purple), Titmice (Tufted), Mourning Doves, Sparrows (House and White-throated)

Hulled Raw Sunflower: Mourning Doves, Sparrows (House)

Feeder-Fillers

Just as bird house design can be used to attract (or exclude) specific species, your feeder's fare can be planned to suit the birds you'd most like to observe.

When trying to cater to birds not listed below, your best guide is the beak shape. A bird's bill is the key to its diet. Note the heavy, seed-cracking beaks of cardinals and finches; the insect-probes of the robin, woodpecker and (most dramatically) woodcock; and the multi-purpose bill of the opportunistic star-

A Versatile Mix

White Proso Millet

Fine Cracked Corn

Black Oil Sunflower

Black Striped Sunflower

Hulled Raw Sunflower

that Fowl Favor

ling. Use these clues to suit your feeder's menu to the patrons you'd most like to attract.

And then, once you've earned a regular clientele, be sure to keep the feeder stocked. Especially in the cold months, when natural sources of food are not available, the sudden shutdown of a feeding station can leave birds stranded, foodless, and in a spot that, were it not for the accustomed bounty of the feeder, they would never have frequented.

Safflower

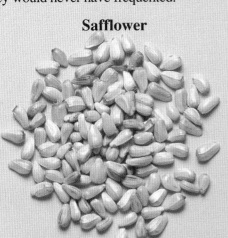

Suet

Hemp Seed

Niger (Thistle)

Raw Peanuts

Fruit Slices

Niger (Thistle): American Goldfinches, Finches (House and Purple), Mourning Doves

Safflower: Cardinals

Raw Peanuts: Blue Jays, Chickadees (Black-capped and Carolina), Finches (House, Green and Purple), Goldfinches (American), Grackles (Common), Grosbeaks (Evening and Rose-breasted), Juncos, Nuthatches (Red- and White-breasted), Sparrows (Field, House and White-Throated), Titmice (Tufted), Wrens (Carolina)

Suet: Blue Birds, Cardinals, Crows, Chickadees (Black-capped and Carolina), Coal tits, Flickers, Goldfinches, Jackdaws, Juncos, Kinglets, Nuthatches (Red- and White-breasted), Thrushes, Titmice (Tufted), Warblers, Woodpeckers (Downy, Hairy, Red-bellied, Red-headed), Wrens

Fruit Slices: Blackbirds, Bluetits, Catbirds, Fieldfares, Orioles (Baltimore, Orchard, Spotted), Redwings, Robins (English), Tanagers (Scarlet, Summer, Western)

Hemp Seed: Finches (House, Chaffinch, Green Finch), Tits, Pipits

Bibliography

Griffin, Paulk, Ed. *The Wood Book*. Montgomery, Alabama: Hatton-Brown Publishers, Inc., 1990.

Hoadley, R. Bruce *Understanding Wood, A Craftsman's Guide to Wood Technology*. Newton, Connecticut: The Taunton Press, Inc., 1980.

Peterson, Roger Tory. *A Field Guide to Birds*. Boston: Houghton Mifflin Co., 1984.

Credits

Bird House Builders: Ralph Schmidt (pgs. 2, 3, 6 bottom, 49, 62, 68, 69, 72, 76, 77, 80, 85, 88, 91, 95, 97, 100, 104, 108, 112, 115, 119, 120); Lee Berry (pgs. 46, 50, 53, 54, 56, 58, 65, 116); Randy Sewell (pgs. 10, 11); Odell Brookshire (pgs. 42, 111); David Schoonmaker (pgs. 40, 110); Rob Pulleyn (p. 43); Garden Source, Atlanta, Georgia (pgs. 14, 45); English Thatch, Inc., Houston, Texas (p. 15); O'Rourke (p. 6 top left); J. Bishop (p. 6 top right); Sontag Rauschke (p. 7 top); D. Holmes (p. 7 bottom); Andy Barnum (p. 8); Steve Bishop (p. 9 top); Dennis Markley (p. 9 bottom); Laura Foreman (p. 12); Thomas Mann (p. 13); Prajna (p. 34); Myatt (p. 35); Betty Clark (p. 36)

Bird House Painters: Shannon Wood (pgs. 49, 62, 68, 69, 76, 77, 80, 88, 91, 95, 97, 104, 108, 120); Michelle Trafton (pgs. 53, 54, 56, 58, 65, 116); Thom Boswell (pgs. 46, 50, 72, 85, 100, 119); Nancy Schoonmaker (p. 38)

Color Consultant: Katherine Long

Accessories: Cheri Jones & Thom Boswell

Bird Feed Consultant: Sally L. Coburn

Museum Credits: Charles A. Wustum Museum, Racine, Wisconsin (pgs. 6-13, 34, 35)

Additional Photography: David Schilling (pgs. 14, 45)

Etchings: Thomas Bewick & his school

Index

METRIC EQUIVALENCY

INCHES	CM
⅛	0.3
¼	0.6
⅜	1.0
½	1.3
⅝	1.6
¾	1.9
⅞	2.2
1	2.5
1¼	3.2
1½	3.8
1¾	4.4
2	5.1
2½	6.4
3	7.6
3½	8.9
4	10.2
4½	11.4
5	12.7
6	15.2
7	17.8
8	20.3
9	22.9
10	25.4
11	27.9
12	30.5
13	33.0
14	35.6
15	38.1
16	40.6
17	43.2
18	45.7
19	48.3
20	50.8
21	53.3
22	55.9
23	58.4
24	61.0
25	63.5
26	66.0
27	68.6
28	71.1
29	73.7
30	76.2
31	78.7
32	81.3
33	83.8
34	86.4
35	88.9
36	91.4
37	94.0
38	96.5
39	99.1
40	101.6
41	104.1
42	106.7
43	109.2
44	111.8
45	114.3
46	116.8
47	119.4
48	121.9
49	124.5
50	127.0

Add interest and character to any room with miniature constructions like this schoolhouse (see page 86).